Beautifully
Resilient

Beautifully Resilient

REDISCOVERING YOURSELF WHEN LIFE DOESN'T GO AS PLANNED

JODI ADCOCK

Publisher iKAN Publish
iKANPublish.com

BEAUTIFULLY RESILIENT
Rediscovering Yourself When Life Doesn't Go As Planned
Jodi Adcock
Certified Life Coach (received training through Coach-U)
Member of the International Coaching Federation (ICF)

I would love to hear from you.
www.beautifullyresilient.com
facebook.com/beautifullyresilient
pinterest.com/beautifullyresilient
@jodi_adcock

ISBN: 13: 978-1975771447
ISBN: 10: 1975771443

Cover and Interior Design: iKAN Publish with Jay Polmar
Cover Photography: Spencer Yates, Eikonapics.com
Butterflies: Jacqueline Roller
Technical Editor: Adam Swiger and Sheri Yates

*H*ello, If you have this book in your hand you or someone you love is struggling with a tough season in life. When I was on my journey to find healing and joy again, I read everything I could get my hands on. I was desperate for knowledge, tools, or anything that could help me. Suffering is not where any of us want to stay for long.

My goal is to provide my readers with tools they can use to persevere and flourish in their rediscovery process. There are seasons in our lives that take us from who we were to who we are now. Retirement, relocation, death in the family, motherhood, empty nest, divorce, disability are to name a few. All of us will eventually struggle with life altering transitions.

> There are seasons in our lives
> that take us from who we were
> to who we are now.

About The Author

You are **Beautifully Resilient!**

*M*y goal is to provide my readers with tools they can use to persevere and flourish in their rediscovery journey. There are seasons in our lives that take us from who we were to who we are now. Retirement, relocation, death in the family, motherhood, empty nest, divorce, disability are to name a few. Most of us struggle with these life-altering transitions.

After struggling through years of infertility, my husband and I made the decision to stop our pursuit for a family. We worked on healing our marriage, relationships with others and our hearts. It took a very long time to feel any joy again. Accepting childlessness was a near impossible feat for me. I had desperately wanted to be a mother and grandmother someday. The loss and sadness was almost too much for me to bear. By the grace of God, I began to piece together a much different life than I knew I could ever have.

Once I came out of my season of suffering, it left me with a desire to walk others through those places in suffering where I know many struggle to push through. I developed Six Levels of Rediscovery. I use these six levels to guide my coaching clients in rediscovering their next season of life and all of its possibilities. This book is your map through that very process. I pray it helps you.

Contents

Introduction

There is a natural progression in life that people hope to experience. You get your education, find a good job, get married, have children, have grandchildren, and retire with enough money to live out the rest of your days in peace. Most people get to see these things come to fruition.

Tragedy can touch our lives at any moment, changing our natural progression into the battle of our lifetime. There are many inspiring stories where individuals exhibit extraordinary perseverance during their season of suffering. But unfortunately, some people will let their tragedy overwhelm and rob them of any joy in the life they have remaining. We do not know how we will prevail in the face of suffering until we are tested.

Years ago, one of the families from the church I attended lost their only child in a horrible car accident. Their eighteen-year-old daughter and a friend of hers were on their way to an event at our church when a truck smashed into them, killing their daughter and critically injuring her friend. That very next Sunday, those grieving parents stood up in front of our entire church congregation to express their sincere thankfulness to God for the blessing of having their daughter.

Around that same time, a couple I knew from my childhood who were still really close to my family had just lost their adult son. He had been shot and killed by a drug dealer. His mother went to her bedroom to cry after hearing the news of her son's death. She stayed in bed for years, as her husband and daughter watched her health slowly decline. It was as if her spirit died that day with her son. These two couples left an impression in my mind of how differently people handle grief and suffering.

It was not until years later, when I personally endured my own season of grief and loss, that I gained a better understanding of how resilience works. It tested me to my very core, and I emerged a different woman. My experience revealed to me many things, like where some individuals can get stuck in their healing process. The mystery of why that mother did not get out of bed became clear, as well as how the other couple could stand in complete gratitude for the years they were given with their daughter. I started to understand a different rhythm of life, the rhythm of rediscovery.

In this book, I lay out six levels to rediscovering your life after a trauma or tragedy. I am not a grief expert only a veteran of it. This model is an effort to gift you with the map that helped me regain my joy. Loss and grief are a part of every human being's life experience. We will all endure suffering, regardless of our spiritual or psychological foundation. Fully understanding what has happened to you is a prerequisite for being able to accept all of the ways that it has changed you. Accepting your reality does not mean you agree with your circumstances. It simply means you can see how suffering has changed you. Accepting that reality is the place where many individuals get stuck. Acceptance usually entails a very long list of changes in your life that you can hardly stand to face.

That is why surrender is so necessary. You eventually get to a place where you have to lay it down. That very long list of things you need to accept in order to start healing will weigh a ton. You will get to the point where you cannot carry it anymore. Until you surrender, healing is impossible. Being able to surrender allows you to breathe again. This little paragraph of wisdom took me many years to figure out.

This is when you start your journey of rediscovering who you are now, because you are different. This is also a place where you can stay and live in discontentment. The choice is yours. If you are interested in living your life to its fullest and rediscovering joy, then I wrote this book for you.

The journey to rediscovery is very difficult. Many people will need to take some time to acclimate to all of the changes, but you can learn to live again and enjoy your life. The human spirit is beautifully resilient. I discovered this after experiencing many years of infertility, which ended in childlessness. I suffered through many years of grief, loss, and depression until one day I found myself able to breathe again.

It took a lot of energy to move past all of that pain. I was eventually able to gather some much-needed tools I used to rediscover the value of my life. This book is the story of my journey and what I learned along the way. I have created six levels, from Suffering to Rediscovery, as a toolset for you to use in your healing process.

The final chapter of this book is for those who are supporting a loved one during a season of suffering. It can be hard to know what to say or how to help a friend who is hurting. I think we all want to live this life to its fullest and not hurt the people we care about, including ourselves.

My prayer is that the tools in
this book will help you find
joy again.

www.beautifullyresilient.com
facebook.com/beautifullyresilient
pinterest.com/beautifullyresilient
@jodi_adcock

Chapter One
Starting a Family

Finding Us...

I met my husband when I was thirty-five years old. My dating life had been a disaster, so I had simply stopped dating for a couple of years prior to meeting him. A friend of mine was hosting a Super Bowl party that year. I walked into that party knowing every person there except that one really good-looking stranger who was sitting on the couch.

His name was John Adcock. He had just moved to Oklahoma that weekend after taking a new job in Oklahoma City. My friend had met John at church that morning and invited him to his Super Bowl party.

Our group of friends all knew one another from the singles' group at our church. Our singles' group met once a week for a Bible study, but we usually ended up going out dancing or meeting for dinner on another night of the week. John started coming to our Bible studies and evenings out on the town, which gave me a chance to get to know him better. He was different from the other guys I had dated. He was an engineer, oddly intelligent, and surprisingly confident. He had definitely stirred my curiosity and interest.

One of our outings involved riding roller coasters at our local theme park one summer afternoon. John and I wandered off by ourselves for most of that day. This was when I knew he was just as interested in getting to know me as I was him. After that day, the two of us started spending more time together. John had just finished having a house built and needed help putting up a fence, landscaping the yard, and a few other tasks. I spent a lot of time at his home helping him with these projects. We would work for several hours, and then he would cook dinner for me to thank me for all of my help. It did not take long for us to start finding other things to do together besides landscaping the yard.

We had both been through some bad dating experiences, so we decided that we would date one another with the purpose of getting married or moving on. We were allowed to ask whatever we wanted to ask one another. The agreement was that we would always give an honest answer. Neither of us wanted to waste any time on the wrong person. I know this sounds kind of like a job interview, but we threw plenty of romance and passion in the mix.

This form of dating worked well for us. After three months of purposeful dating, John proposed. We were married on April 3, 2009, in a beautiful historic ballroom by my cousin Jason and my brother Scott, who were both pastors. It was lovely.

The morning after our wedding, we were off to the Grand Cayman Islands. Once John had proposed to me, he asked if I would get certified in scuba diving. He had been scuba diving since he was a teenager and loved it. He really wanted us to enjoy diving together. So in the three months I had to plan our wedding, I was also trying to pack up my house and get certified in scuba diving. It was an intense three months. Our honeymoon was a beautiful place to recover from the hustle, but went by too fast. However, I was excited to return to our home together as John and Jodi Adcock.

It was strange to change my last name. I had been Jodi Morris for thirty-five years. I had never been a wife before. This felt different, more intense. I had a clear vision of the kind of wife I aspired to be; I would be protective, encouraging, self-sacrificing ... as long as he did not tell me what I could or could not do, say, or buy.

Learning how to live in union with someone is not for sissies. Being an independent woman, who had taken care of herself for years, made it very difficult to let my husband even change a light bulb. I knew how to change my own light bulb. I knew how to do a lot of things. I had to learn to let my husband do certain things for me. His idea of being a good husband was to take care of me.

There were many life lessons in those first few months of marriage. It was a rough start.

Finn...

Despite the struggles we had those first few months, I was so in love with my husband and wanted to make several babies with him. I was in my mid-thirties and could hear my biological clock ticking. John and I both wanted children and thought that two kids would be perfect. We felt like we were too far down life's path to outnumber ourselves. We hoped for one boy and one girl.

One morning I woke up with horrible pain in my hip joints, and my mouth tasted like metal. I got ready and went to work thinking whatever weirdness was happening would eventually go away. But, after a few hours at work, my symptoms did not go away. I was telling one of my coworkers about the metal taste in my mouth. She giggled and said, "You're pregnant."

It had never occurred to me that I might be pregnant. The thought of being pregnant made me feel nauseated and a type of joyful anxiety at the same time. I had to know if I was pregnant as soon as possible.

Next door to the place I was working was a minor emergency clinic, so I walked over and asked a nurse friend of mine there to draw my blood for a quick pregnancy test. A few minutes later, she came back in with a big smile on her face, saying "Congratulations."

I knew the second I walked back into work that all of my coworkers would want to know the results, but I wanted John to be the first to know. So without much thought, I text him, "I'm pregnant." I later realized that was not the best way to tell your husband he's going to be a father for the first time. He called me immediately to tell me that very thing and to let me know how happy he was. We were both a little freaked out by the news, but also really excited.

We called our family and closest friends that night to share our good news. We quickly became those annoying first-time parents who could only talk about baby stuff. Our conversations were consumed with topics like good baby names, how to decorate the nursery, what school district we wanted to live in, family traditions we wanted to start or continue, what birthing classes we should take, etc.

> *Children are a gift from the*
> *LORD; they are a reward*
> *from him.*
>
> *—Psalm 127:3*

It is such a strange, joyous feeling to be pregnant. I was growing another human being inside of my body. A couple of weeks into my pregnancy, I began to experience some cramping. I had read about how the uterus can stretch during pregnancy and cause cramping. I had experienced hip-joint pain on and off, so I just assumed the cramping was normal. I knew my pregnancy was still early, so I tried to drown out any fears I was having with hope, faith, and prayer.

I decided to call my doctor and let her check me out just to be safe. My doctor checked my HCG levels and told me to come back a couple of days later to have them rechecked. She explained that the placenta produces the HCG hormone and my HCG number should double every a couple of days.

My husband had to travel out of state for a business meeting. Everything seemed to be progressing normally, so we decided that he should go ahead and keep his plans to go out of town. It was only a few hours after he had left that morning when the intense cramping started.

I knew something was wrong. I called my cousin who had experienced a miscarriage several years ago to ask her about my symptoms. She was very concerned and sent her brother over to pick me up to take me to the emergency room. I called my doctor to let her know that I was on my way to the ER.

My doctor met us there. An ultrasound revealed that my pregnancy was ectopic. My baby was lodged in my fallopian tube, and the tube had begun to tear. My doctor's words echoed in my heart "Your fallopian tube needs to be surgically removed, or it will rupture."

She forgot to include my baby in that statement. I was informed that I would be prepped for surgery in the next few minutes. Time stood still.

But, everything kept happening. My cousin called my husband to deliver the tragic news. John was stuck at the airport trying to get home. There was nothing he could do. It broke my heart for him not to get to be there with me.

> **Time sort of stood still for me in that moment.**

It was my first surgery and I was so scared. The nurse asked me to undress and put on a surgery gown, hat, and shoes. My clothes were placed into a bag. An anesthesiologist came in and asked me several questions about any allergies I might have to certain medications. He told me what he was going to give me. My hospital room quickly filled up with family members who prayed over me as the nurses took me back to the surgery room.

RULE #1

Make sure you have people in your life that will help you in your time of need.

When I woke up in the recovery room, tears filled my eyes as my heart broke. I immediately felt the loss of my baby. My family had all gone home. My brother stayed so that he could take me home once I recovered and was released from the hospital. My brother stayed with me at my house until John got home later that evening. My mind kept repeating, "This really happened." It was surprising to me how much love I had for our baby after only having him with me for a just few short weeks.

Finn Harrison Adcock

September 2009

The morning after my surgery, I was sitting in a chair outside in the backyard watching my husband pull weeds from our flower beds. My activity was restricted until I healed from the laparoscopic surgery. The sun felt comforting and healing to me. It was like a warm hug that melted away all of my sadness.

Our friends Brian and Kristy stopped by to announce some good news. They were so excited to tell us that they were pregnant as well. They did not know about my surgery and that we had just lost our baby. It was an awkward moment for all of us as we tried to show happiness for them at the same time they expressed their condolences for our loss.

Brian and Kristy had a son named Noah. To this day, every time I see Noah, I am reminded of how old Finn would have been.

Mia...

Several days later, as I was lying in bed staring at the ceiling, I suddenly recalled a conversation I had with a good friend of mine that previous year. My friend had experienced a miscarriage, and in my effort to comfort her, I told her that the baby most likely had something wrong with it. In my present state of mind, I could not believe I had said something so insensitive and hurtful to her. Guilt flooded my heart as I now understood the gravity of her pain. I called her immediately and apologized. Thankfully, she forgave me. I was so ignorant to the profound loss a woman feels after a miscarriage.

Over the next few months, our friends and family had begun to ask when we were going to try again. The truth was that we had never stopped. It had simply taken my body several months to get pregnant. We were cautiously excited about this second pregnancy. My OB/GYN had referred us to a high-risk pregnancy specialist because I was over the age of thirty-five. Although that made me feel like an old lady trying to have a baby, it was comforting to be with a doctor who regularly dealt with challenging pregnancies.

Our specialist watched me closely over the next several weeks. I had appointments scheduled every two to three days to check on my HCG levels. These levels were supposed to be almost doubling at every check-up, but mine had barely increased from the last few times they had been tested. Fear filled every ounce of me as I fought to stay positive and hopeful. The next couple of weeks were excruciating. There were many blood tests, ultrasounds, and emotions. Then, something familiar started happening to me. I began to cramp and experience symptoms of miscarrying.

I recalled a story I had read in the Bible about a woman named Hannah. In 1 Samuel 1:27, she prayed for a child. She was barren and desperately wanted to be a mother. She cried out in such desperation to the Lord that a local priest overhearing her thought she was drunk and carrying on. When she explained to the priest her situation, he said, "Go in peace, and may the God of Israel grant you what you have asked of him." The Lord granted her a son, and she named him Samuel. I fell on my knees to plead with God in the same way Hannah had plead for her child. With desperation and tears, I cried out to God to help my body not miscarry my baby. I felt an undeniable comfort from God at that very moment. But, I knew I would not be able to keep my baby. I told God that I felt like Peter (in Matthew 14:22–33) standing on that ocean with Jesus and sinking due to my lack of faith. God reminded me that He did not allow Peter to drown and He would do the same for me.

Mia Sienna Adcock

March 2010

Josiah...

My heart still felt pregnant, but my brain was painfully aware that I had miscarried. It was strange for me to experience intense emotions contrary to my reality. My body still wanted to be pregnant, so the very next chance it got, it made a baby. I was pregnant again only a few weeks later.

My doctor warned me that this pregnancy could not sustain itself due to my recent miscarriage. My uterine lining was not strong enough. However, I read so many stories online of women who had gotten pregnant immediately after a miscarriage and went on to have successful pregnancies. A few of my friends shared stories with me of women they knew who had done the same. I hoped my doctor was wrong.

One of the hardest days of my infertility was sitting in my doctor's office waiting for confirmation of what I already knew to be true: I was experiencing another miscarriage. I sat in that waiting room for over an hour watching so many smiling happy couples come and go with their families gathered around them and ultrasound photographs in hand. I tried desperately to choke back my tears, as they streamed down my face. I hid my face behind a magazine, impatiently waiting for my nightmare to come to an end.

John had asked me if I needed him to go with me, but I told him no. He would always start by saying how busy he was, and then ask if I needed him there. He could cancel this or that and get someone to cover. I always felt guilty asking him to come with me. The truth is that we had both been in denial of our circumstances and it did not matter if John was there, or anyone else. I knew it would still hurt just as much. I was pretty angry that the receptionist did not put me in a room to wait instead of leaving me to contend with all of the happy pregnant people. My veterinarian did not abandon me in the lobby when I euthanized my dog. I expected the same consideration here. That week, I miscarried my third baby.

Josiah was only in my womb for five weeks before we lost him.

Josiah Glen Adcock

April 2010

——•••——

Chapter Two
Infertility

I started to feel like my body was killing my babies. I had experienced one ectopic pregnancy and two miscarriages. We had lost three babies in a very short time period. We wanted a baby so badly. I prayed and prayed that God would heal my body. My biological clock started to get louder and louder. I felt as if I were quickly running out of time. I worried that there was something wrong with my body. I needed some answers.

Our high-risk pregnancy doctor referred us to a Reproductive Endocrinologist (RE). My RE wanted to do a hysterosalpingogram on me, which would flush dye through my remaining fallopian tube while viewing it with an ultrasound to check for blockages. Did I mention, this was done without anesthesia? Unfortunately, my fallopian tube was all crinkled up and the pressure from the dye flushing through it sort of straightened it out.

This procedure was ridiculously painful. I thought I had a pretty high pain tolerance until this, but I should have had a stick to bite down on for this procedure. Instead, I almost broke my husband's hand gripping it so tightly.

After the procedure, the RE asked if I had ever run a high fever for an extended period of time. I recalled years before becoming very sick from salmonella poisoning, during which my fever ran high for several days. I thought I was sick with the flu, so put off seeking medical attention. I ended up going to the emergency room, where I spent several days in the hospital. It could have been that time or a few times when I had kidney infections or ear infections as a kid. None of the people in my family have ever been good about going to the doctor. We always practiced this mindset that we just needed to drink plenty of water and sleep it off.

My RE explained that any prolonged high fever could have damaged my fallopian tubes since all of my other tests were normal. My RE advised us that in-vitro fertilization (IVF) was our best option for a successful pregnancy. Or we could roll the dice, go home, and make another effort to conceive the natural way. He had opened up my remaining fallopian tube a little during the hysterosalpingogram. John and I discussed it for a few days and decided our chances of achieving pregnancy seemed safer with in-vitro fertilization since there was still a risk of an ectopic pregnancy.

Our RE required us to attend a class on IVF before we got started. It was a basic overview of the process of in-vitro fertilization. I had heard so many horror stories of women losing their minds and tempers during IVF hormone therapy, so John and I came up with names for the different emotions I might experience. We thought this might help in advance to separate me from the effects the hormones might have on my personality. We came up with Psycho Sally, Needy Norma, and Mopey Molly. We later added Dopey Debbie because we needed her.

We had so many hard and bizarre conversations over the next few weeks on topics like whether my husband was able to inject me with a needle over and over again, whether I was comfortable with my husband going into "the special room" and masturbating to something outside of our marriage for a semen specimen, whether we would tell our child about his or her conception, and what the hormone manipulation would do to my body long-term. John and I felt that we should decide how far we were willing to go with IVF. We decided that if we did not get pregnant after trying IVF twice, then we would assume God's answer was "No." The topic of adoption was also mentioned. We had both heard horrific stories associated with adoption. Both of us really did not want to entertain that topic. We had enough in front of us to deal with.

———— •●• ————

Benjie and Arianna...

Our friends and family had many questions for us regarding IVF as well. Some of the comments and concerns were funny, and others were simply unreal because they were so offensive. An acquaintance of ours informed me that she thought "IVF was the closest thing to playing God she could think of." Of course, she had children already. But, most of our friends and family were supportive. We only had to bury a couple of people.

Understanding all of the complexities surrounding IVF was overwhelming. IVF was not one of those things we could just let the doctor do for us. The process required us to order all medications, syringes, and other supplies to ensure we would have enough to last throughout the entire process. We calculated out how many milliliters we would need of each medication over the next three months. If I ran out of a medication, it would take weeks to get more. IVF only works if you take the medications exactly like you are supposed to. Having to reorder medications was simply not an option. Once the process started, it must continue.

We had to educate ourselves on the possible side effects, injection sites, and so many other things that could potentially influence our outcome. We received a large box at the front door one day full of vials, syringes, alcohol swabs, biohazard containers, and an Epi-pen for emergency reactions. What we were about to put ourselves through was a bit intimidating.

My RE started me with a thirty-day round of birth control pills. Shortly afterwards, the shots began. I tried to stay focused on seeing the face of my baby and all of the sweet moments motherhood had in store for me. That focus made me brave in the face of all of those shots and hormones.

RULE #2

If you can't say
something nice,
say nothing at all.

The next step was a once a day injection of Lupron in my stomach. Thankfully, these were tiny syringes and the medication was not painful. This was not a bad start. The functions of these two meds were to drop my estrogen levels, which should take about thirty days. Unfortunately, I had formed a large cyst on one of my ovaries that was keeping my levels from dropping. To combat the cyst, my RE put me on a medication called Norethindrone. It had a few side effects like nausea, headaches, dizziness, mood swings, trouble sleeping, weight loss, breast swelling, and tenderness. I felt every one of those side effects. The good news was that it worked quickly.

My RE's nurse did not tell me that the lack of estrogen would make my brain stop working. One day my estrogen dropped so low that I got lost driving home from work. I ended up having to pull over and call John so that he could talk me home. My husband found the milk in the cabinet one morning and cereal in the fridge. I experienced several of these brainless moments. This period in our lives was hilarious and a little scary.

Once my estrogen had dropped to the desired level, we moved onto stimulation drugs. This was when it started to suck. This was a combination of two different drugs. IVF hormone suppression of estrogen felt like going through extreme menopause over a thirty-day period, and then the stimulation drugs instantly turned my body into a horny, pimple-faced, thirteen-year-old girl. Not that I could or even wanted to have sex during this time. I had forgotten how bewitching hormones were in such high concentrations. My bad choices and fierce passion for everything not good for my body dominated my mind. The stimulation drugs made my ovaries the size of grapefruits. They were normally the size of walnuts. It was uncomfortable physically and emotionally, to say the least.

The stimulation drugs were syrupy and thick, and required larger needles. One of the drugs called Repronex burned during injection and left large red welts around my belly button. It was hard to find a place to inject that did not hurt. I usually had an ice pack or heating pad on my stomach during this time. I tried to stay focused on the reason for the season. Two months later, my ovaries were full of eggs. We had met our goal. Every egg was an opportunity for a baby.

We were ready for the best part: retrieval and conception. We were excited to hear that my RE was able to collect twenty eggs out of my thirty-eight-year-old body during the retrieval procedure. That was an impressive number of eggs. The eggs went into the lab with the embryologist, where they were injected with my husband's sperm. Then *poof!*—we had twenty little lives. This was an overwhelming realization.

Over the next five days, our lab tech (we referred to as our babysitter) called us with daily updates on how the little ones were developing. My RE wanted Grade A embryos and nothing below a Grade C. We sat on pins and needles for five days. The waiting process was excruciating. By the third day, the lab tech called to report that we had two "Grade A" embryos to transfer to my uterus. We could not believe that out of our twenty, only two were Grade A. We felt a strange sadness and loss for the other embryos that did not develop.

Around day five, our two embryos were ready to be put back in my womb. The procedure to transfer the embryos only took a few minutes. We also had gotten news that one other embryo had simply been a late bloomer, so we decided to cryo-freeze it for the time being. Placing two embryos in my uterus could possibly produce twins or triplets, so two was my RE's maximum. We would come back and have the frozen embryo transferred into my womb at a later date. We lovingly referred to this embryo as our Snowbaby.

We had to wait nine days to know whether or not our embryos had implanted into my uterus resulting in pregnancy. Those nine days went by so very slow. It seemed as though time was deliberating trying to stop. On that ninth day, the minutes felt like days to us. Finally, we got the call. We were pregnant. Our HCG levels were notably high, meaning we might be pregnant with twins. I had a mild panic attack thinking about the possibility of raising twins in the midst of my joyful tears.

Over the next few weeks, things were going well. The thought of being pregnant with twins was so exciting. I imagined every little twin thing that I could make, have, and buy. Although I really wanted to, I would not let myself set up a nursery until the second trimester. But, my mental decorator was very busy playing with same-sex versus opposite-sex twin decor.

One morning, I woke up experiencing some intense cramping. My RE had me come in for an examination. His tests revealed that one of the embryos had implanted itself in my remaining fallopian tube. I had another ectopic pregnancy. When my RE had placed our embryos back in my uterus, one embryo had swum up into my fallopian tube and snuggled in for development. My RE explained to me that there is less than a 1% chance of this happening. Go figure.

The fallopian tube had begun to tear, so I was scheduled for surgery that next morning. I was so focused on what had to be done that I was not able to process what was actually happening. My RE removed my only remaining fallopian tube, along with our baby.

I found myself in a very confused state of mind over the several days following my surgery. My doctor kept having me come in for blood draws to check my HCG levels. I thought I was still pregnant with the other baby. It had not occurred to me that I would lose both of them. When I started cramping and bleeding heavily, I realized my body was miscarrying the other baby.

I called my mom to tell her the news and she reacted with frustration and anger. She insisted that I misunderstood the doctor and then asked how the nurse knew for sure that I had miscarried the other baby. Her emotional response was so out of character and odd. It was apparent to me that she was exhibiting frustration in her denial. My dad had also called a couple of times over those next few days crying to me over the loss of his grandbabies. I started to become aware of the pain my choices were putting my family through. I have always been very close with both of my parents. I can only imagine the heartbreak a parent feels watching their child suffer from any pain. There was a lot of energy and emotion swirling all around me and inside of me.

Time seemed to stand still for me over the next several days as I stared into nothingness with a steady stream of tears rolling down my cheeks. The tears just would not stop. My dogs were concerned about me. They were very clingy, cuddling me and offering lots of kisses. It took several weeks for me to be able to function normally again. My body healed slowly from that second surgery. The carbon dioxide gas that resulted from my procedure created a lot of discomfort in my body. It took a couple of weeks for my body to absorb it all. The three tiny sutured cuts on my abdomen were a reminder to me that a part of my body was no longer with me. I no longer had fallopian tubes and I now felt like 99% of a person.

Benjamin Dale Adcock

Arianna Elise Adcock

August 2010

Ethan, Sophia, and Rose...

My RE recommended that we not wait too long to pursue another round of IVF. I was not ready emotionally to go back for another attempt. But, I felt like I needed to follow my RE's instructions. IVF would be my only hope of achieving pregnancy after the removal of both fallopian tubes. Three months after my surgery, we started our second round of IVF. That big box full of syringes with vials of hormones was sitting on my front porch once more. That naive anticipation I once had was gone for this round of IVF. I knew what to expect and what the risks were. It was difficult to put my family and friends through that entire process of watching and waiting all over again. We all desperately wanted the same results. I would be giving myself 265 shots over the next three months in the hopes of making us parents, as well as adding endearing titles to my loving family members.

In the midst of all of this, we noticed that the grout in our kitchen was looking darker. John asked me if I had spilled anything on the floor. After ruling out all of the possible reasons for grout suddenly getting darker, we opened up our lower cabinets to discover a massive covering of mold along the entire wall of our lower kitchen cabinets. Apparently, we had a slow water leak somewhere. We contacted our insurance agent knowing this was going to be a significant repair. Our agent put us in contact with a building contractor he knew and trusted.

Suddenly, our house was full of people pulling out our kitchen cabinets and knocking out walls. I could stand in my living room and see through the kitchen and utility room into our garage. I now had the daunting task of making sure half of the house was reconstructed correctly. Our poor dogs were so nervous and completely stressed out about the loud noises and strangers in our house. They spent most of the day hiding under our bed. The chaos in the house elevated the stress levels in all of us.

My husband's workload considerably increased when his responsibilities doubled in size. Although it was busy and added more stress, John's bosses noticed how well he managed both areas and decided to promote him. This was thrilling news but came with a caveat: we would have to relocate to Shreveport, Louisiana, for a couple of years. The contractors had to finish up so we could start packing and put the house up for sale.

All of that would have to wait because it was time for our RE to take me into surgery to collect as many eggs as he could from my ovaries. My RE had to pass a long needle through my vaginal wall into each ovary removing the eggs one by one. The procedure took about fifteen minutes with an hour and a half of recovery time. My eggs were once again handed off to the embryologist to work her magic. We would have to wait five long days to hear how many of our embryos survived the laboratory process. The daily updates from our embryologist (aka babysitter) helped ease my intense maternal feelings.

The RE had retrieved eight eggs from my ovaries. The embryologist injected all eight, but only three survived. Five days later, those three embryos were transferred back in my uterus.

Back to our house news, one of the carpenters had found black mold inside the walls. It worried me because I had heard that black mold was dangerous to inhale. Our building contractor called in a mold cleaning service to handle the problem.

While wearing bio-hazard suits, the mold removing crew hung plastic everywhere. My house looked like that scene from the movie E.T. where the government finally catches E.T. and takes over Eliot's house. Mold spores were captured and placed into specimen jars to be analyzed later. They meticulously tore out all of the sheetrock with black mold, which stirred up the mold spores. All of the construction had to be postponed for a couple of weeks. They treated it like asbestos. It seemed a little over the top to me. If I had not been trying to have a baby, I would have sprayed it with bleach and called it good.

Because of the black mold spores and the possibility I could be pregnant, we were required to stay in a hotel with our dogs. The hotel elevators were broken, which meant I was walking leashed dogs up and down the stairs for their bathroom breaks. I was worried that the embryos would not implant with all of the stress and the dogs yanking me around by their leashes. The entire mold clean-up process was ridiculous and expensive. We were informed that we would need proof that our house was now "mold free" before the reconstruction could continue and we could place it on the market. The mold company did finally let me back in, but I was quarantined to the bedroom. We still had plastic sheets hanging everywhere with HEPA vacuums running all over the house.

Our nine days of waiting was over and we were awaiting our pregnancy phone call results once more. Our family and friends were anxious with us. I started experiencing intense feelings of guilt, knowing that I was putting our family and friends through all of this with us because I wanted to be pregnant and have my own children. It made me feel incredibly selfish.

My parents desperately wanted to be grandparents. I have an older brother with two children, but he and my dad had a horrible falling out several years ago, which resulted in a fractured relationship. My dad and step mom rarely, if ever, saw my brother's children. My dad and step mom were just as desperate for grandchildren as we were for children. That unintended pressure made the loss of each pregnancy even harder to handle. It made me feel like I was letting them down.

Every time I had gotten pregnant before, my hip joints would hurt and I would taste metal in my mouth for the first few days of pregnancy. I had not felt any symptoms of pregnancy this time around. John and I had agreed before starting IVF that we would only attempt it twice, so this was my last opportunity to be pregnant, give birth, and all of the million other things I wanted to experience.

John came home from work early on this day so we could be together to receive our 4 p.m. phone call. The nurse called and delivered the news. We were not pregnant. My pregnancy test was negative. I will never forget John's reaction that day. He sat on the edge of the bed for about an hour saying to himself, "Now what do we do?" over and over again. It was so heartbreaking for me to see him that upset. The unbearable sadness of this day forever changed us. We did not even discuss the loss. We just threw ourselves back into our current circumstances – finish the house, packing, and moving.

Ethan Lucas Adcock

Sophia Elise Adcock

Rosalie Harper Adcock

December 2010

Chapter Three
Now What

My Sweet Mazzie...

W hile I was running dogs up and down stairs at the hotel, my thirteen-year-old dog Mazzie had been experiencing abdominal pain and some labored breathing. Her veterinary visit revealed a large tumor on her spleen. Mazzie had not ever been my pet; she was more like a roommate. It had just been us two girls for years before John came into our lives. She was my dearest friend and I loved her beyond words.

She was the kind of dog that understood English, human gestures, and emotions. She was smart, unique, and the sweetest fuzzy friend ever. Her cancer spread fast and was painful for her.

The veterinarian had told me that he could try to remove her spleen surgically, but it would be risky for a dog her age. Once he opened her up to remove her spleen, if the cancer had spread, he would not wake her up from the surgery. After much discussion, we decided not to do the surgery. We decided to let her live out her days until the pain became too much for her.

Mazzie collapsed to the floor and yelped in pain only a few days later. I cried and cried. I felt so helpless in my inability to make her better. She seemed to recover quickly acting normal over the next several days. Then it happened again. She collapsed to the floor crying out. This time she stayed down for a while, whimpering in pain.

Because I loved her entirely too much to allow her to suffer, I called John at work and asked if he could meet me at our veterinarian's office. We made the most painful decision to euthanize her that day. There were no words for the depth of pain my heart was suffering at this time. We had gotten the negative pregnancy test the previous week. This period was a bit hazy for me. There was too much sadness in such a short period of time.

———— •●• ————

The Aftermath...

Next thing I knew we were living in a two-bedroom apartment in Shreveport with Kaiser our two-year-old boxer. My husband was so busy with his new position that he was gone a lot of the time. I was wrapping up things with the contractors at our house in Oklahoma so that I could get it sold, as well as trying to find a new house to purchase in Shreveport. I had to quit my job in Oklahoma, so I was also trying to find a new job in a new town. Our wonderful real estate agent in Oklahoma was kind enough to take over getting our house sold for us. She was successful in doing so only a few months later. We were thrilled to have one less thing to worry about.

Our time in the apartment was crazy. John threw himself into work while I fell apart. It became harder and harder for me to cope with my days. I was continuously job searching and house hunting. Every evening John and I fought over my inability to accomplish these two seemingly simple tasks. I felt like he was punishing me for not being able to give him children. I was so lost in emotion and desperately needed him to stop yelling at me. Our fights escalated into cussing and throwing things at one another, which added shame to my long list of emotions.

I had never fought like this with anyone throughout my life. I felt so embarrassed and deeply saddened by these arguments. There was one evening when John said some intensely harsh things to me, and I retaliated by picking up a stapler and baseballing it at his head. Thankfully, it only stuck in the sheetrock instead. These were not good times.

Our dog Kaiser was missing Mazzie and his large backyard. He was now stuck in an apartment with two emotionally dysfunctional adults. Our fighting was too much for all of us. Kaiser started losing his hair and vomiting from time to time. He was so sweet and loving to me during the day while John was gone. When John came home from work, Kaiser would hide in the back bedroom. I hated this for him. I hated it for all of us. I kept thinking things had to get better soon. Perhaps it would after we were able to move into a house and got out of that tiny apartment.

I was fortunate enough to hire a fantastic real estate agent in Shreveport. About once a week, she would come by our apartment to pick me up so we would go look at two or three houses. Afterward, we would usually grab lunch. It was nice for me to meet someone that was a caring and a nonjudgmental listener. This wonderful woman practiced true kindness with me, becoming a dear friend.

After a few months of looking at houses, I finally found one that fit our lifestyle. It was a cute little three-bedroom with the most gorgeous screened porch off the back of the house. The screened porch had a beautifully landscaped pergola-covered patio complete with a decorative pond and waterfall. I could see me sipping tea on that screened porch and enjoying its serenity, and

I needed peace. The backyard was a nice size. Big enough for Kaiser to run and play. We decided to buy it.

Packing and moving again was a nice distraction from all of our unhealed wounds. We settled into our home. All seemed to be going well. We thought it was time to get Kaiser a playmate. We could at least make our dog happy, even if we were not.

We added another baby boxer to our family we named Stella. She was a little black and white boxer, also known as sealed brindle. She was so adorable. It felt good for all of us to be able to love on that sweet little puppy. Kaiser and Stella would play for hours together on the floor while John and I watched and laughed. There was some joy in our house again. Every time John sat in his recliner, Stella had to lay on his chest. She loved John. She was so healing for us.

———•●•———

Adoption...

Because of my deep longing to be a mother, I tried to talk to John about adoption. He was hesitant about adoption but agreed to go with me to visit the adoption center in Shreveport. We sat down with a very nice lady and asked her five million questions. We were both encouraged by the process when we left. We found out that one of the elders from our church was an adoption attorney who had worked with the same adoption center for many years. He had inspiring things to say about her and the adoption center. This was good.

It was a common occurrence in our church for someone to stand in front of the congregation and give their testimony of how they had seen God move in their lives. That same elder got up in front of the church one Sunday to speak about the joy and struggles he had experienced being an adoption attorney.

He told a story about a family who had adopted a baby from a young single mother. After a few months had gone by, the birth father showed up demanding parental rights to his baby. The birth mother had claimed not to know the birth father's identity. A paternity test verified the father's biological rights to his baby. The family who had adopted this baby, and taken it into their home and hearts as their own, were forced by the courts to hand the baby over to its biological father.

This story created so much fear in my husband's heart that he became permanently opposed to adoption. John did not share with me how much this story had affected him at this time. He refused to talk about adoption it at all. I assumed that he was taking time to heal from all of our loss, because anytime I brought up the topic of adoption, it would quickly turn into an argument. I was frustrated that he would not have this discussion with me. When we had left the adoption center, we both seemed to be on the same page, but then he just shut it all down. I did not understand. On one occasion when I tried forcing this talk, he yelled "Am I not enough for you?" It silenced me.

Over time, the arguments escalated and I could not emotionally or physically handle any more conflict. So, I decided to leave my husband. I had to go somewhere peaceful and think. If my husband did not want to adopt, then it would just be the two of us. I needed to know if that was enough for me. We had a painfully challenging marriage. I needed to decide if I would sacrifice ever being a mother for a man who was so angry toward me. I packed up my Jeep along with the dogs and went home to Oklahoma. I stayed with family for a few days before leasing a house.

John and I had seen several marriage counselors throughout the years. We seemed to have the same ongoing issues in which no counselor could help. When John got emotional, he yelled, and it made my brain shut down. I needed him to stop yelling, and he just needed me to listen. It was our perpetual insanity.

After our many fights throughout our marriage, we never apologized to one another or had any kind of making up time. Our routine was to just not talk for a couple of days, then act like it never happened. I knew this was not healthy, but for the life of me, I did not have a clue how to make it better. There were times when I simply needed to get away from him.

My commitment to my marriage was something I took very seriously and it sustained us through many tough times. I had vowed to love this man for better or worse in front of our family and friends and God, but I had just left him. My leaving him only made him angrier. We attempted to discuss matters over the phone a few times, but he quickly raised his voice and I could not listen to one more second of it. It did not take long before we stopped talking altogether. This was a very dark time; I felt absolutely alone in my suffering. I had lost my children and my husband. I spent a good portion of my time crying on the sofa, curled up with my two dogs. None of us were happy.

It was several weeks before we got our second wind and were able to have a constructive conversation. John and I finally realized that we deeply loved each other and we both wanted our marriage to work. After many discussions over the next several weeks, John asked me to come home. Up until that moment, I was not sure if he wanted to be married or wanted to move on from the nightmare our marriage had been for him. It was good to know he loved me and still wanted to be my husband. John drove to Oklahoma and moved all of us back home to live with him in Shreveport.

I think it took those couple of months of separation for us to get our heads and hearts straight. Neither of us was fully aware of the grief and loss we were both enduring. My husband's heartache was expressed in frustration and anger. My heartache showed up in depression and the need to escape.

RULE #3

Marriage is not for sissies.
You will have to fight for it.

The enormous amount of pain we had experienced in such a short period resulted in grief overload. We had lost eight babies over the past fifteen months. It was just too much loss. We were relieved that we had not lost our marriage as well.

———•••———

Elisha, Liam, and Olivia...

John really needed for us to try to move on with our lives. We needed to escape from the world of continually working to have children. It was painful for me to wrap my mind around the idea that I would never be a mother. My last hope was our one frozen embryo that had been in cryostorage since our first IVF cycle. We felt obligated to give this baby a chance at life. After much discussion, we decided to adopt two other embryos to increase our chances of pregnancy.

A couple that had gotten pregnant with twins during their first IVF cycle had donated these two embryos so that a couple like us could adopt them. When you choose to undergo the process of IVF, the embryos and the parents are tested for several chromosomal defects. We were fortunate enough to have important genetic information about these embryos and their parents.

The world of IVF and genetics was just strange science for most of our family and friends. I remember trying to explain to one of my family members that we were adopting embryos, and about the testing the embryos had undergone. That person blurted out their objection by telling me that "Hitler had done the same thing when he tried to create his perfect race."

They later called back to apologize. But the damage was already done. The comment was so harsh that I started to question if God approved of what I was doing. I wondered if I was taking all of it too far, or if I was even a good person. A long cry, and a reasonable conversation with my accountability partner and dear friend, put my mind at ease and back on track.

The embryo transfer went well. It was the longest nine days of our lives—waiting for our very last pregnancy test results.

The test was negative. This loss had another component of grief with it. I had adopted another mother's embryos and lost them as well. I asked my doctor's nurse to contact the mother of those embryos and let her know. I hope she actually called that mother. She needed to know that her children were not out there in the world somewhere or still frozen.

Elisha Nathaniel Adcock

Liam Tobias Adcock

Olivia Frances Adcock

July 2012

Trying to Move On...

John and I had begun to make plans to buy land and build a house once we moved back to Oklahoma. I think it was our way of trying to move on. Every Friday evening we would go out to eat and discuss what kind of house we wanted. I had begun to spend quite a bit of my time on Pinterest finding pictures of styles of houses we liked. Every trip back to Oklahoma included looking for land. This was a refreshing distraction from the sadness and grief. It made a little room for hope in our future.

One of the friends I had made in Shreveport enjoyed kayaking the Red River from time to time. She called me one day to tell me about a strange and wonderful experience she had on the river that day. She had met a young woman on the river who seemed to be upset and crying. She paddled over to check on her. The woman explained that she was not married and had recently found out she was pregnant. She dreamed of a career in the military and never wanted children, so she had decided to give the baby up for adoption.

My friend immediately thought of John and me. She told the woman about our story in trying to have a baby. It all seemed fortuitous. I was sitting in the Target parking lot when she called to tell me every detail about her encounter with this young woman. My friend just knew that God was using her to help us get a baby. When I hung up from our call, I cried uncontrollably for about thirty minutes in my car before I could pull myself together enough to drive home. I did not bother to mention the conversation to John until several days later. I knew he was closed to adoption and it would only cause an argument. I called my friend a few days later to let her know how sweet she was to think of us, but we were not interested in meeting with the young woman.

The finality of our efforts to have children left me with deep sadness. Honestly, even if John had been open to adoption, it would have been hard for me to care for a baby with the level of grief I needed to process. We had spent our entire marriage trying to have a baby. I needed to try to heal so that I could breathe again. I also wanted to get my marriage back to a healthy place. We needed to restore our lives and attempt to move on.

Oklahoma...

My husband and I returned home to Oklahoma, after being in Shreveport for almost three years. The move back had its challenges. A town a few miles south of our hometown of Edmond was a town called Moore that had just recently experienced a severe tornado. Because of the masses of people without homes, all of the homes for lease in Edmond were rented the second they became available. We called our friend and real estate agent, who had sold our house for us before we left, and asked for her help. She was able to find us a home to lease quickly. We would miss all of the sweet friends we had made in

Shreveport. But, it was comforting to move back home to be near our friends and family once again.

A few months after being back in Oklahoma, my husband and I purchased ten acres with a beautiful pond on it and then started the process of building our dream home. People kept telling us that building a house could be hard for a marriage. I worried about that at first. With everything we had gone through, I was cautious about anything that could be harmful to our marriage.

We actually enjoyed the process of building our house. It was fun for us to see all of our date night planning come into existence. We built a large shop where my husband could restore his old cars and several garden beds for all of my plants. Building this house was so personal for me. There was not one cabinet knob, piece of tile, or slab of wood that I had not personally picked out. I could walk through that house while it was still being framed and see the finished look. That makes it almost impossible for the builder, but he did the best we could to make our dream come to life. We love our home and the land we have been blessed to own. I feel protective and responsible for both.

———•••———

Living with Childlessness...

Every day I think of something that I would have loved to show my children or share with them. The blue herring hunting frogs on our pond, the baby turtles we found in our outdoor kitchen, all of the pretty flowers, and so many other things. Not to mention the moments piled up on the sofa watching a movie or the summers spent swimming in the pool. I could go on and on. Grief seems to live right under your skin for a while, until it settles into your bones. Grief never goes away; you just find a place inside of yourself for it to live where it will not be too disruptive to your life.

I had a friend ask me if I am glad I do not have kids now, because I have the freedom to go and do anything I want. I told her that I will never stop wanting to have kids. A woman does not put herself through over five hundred injections, several invasive procedures, plus the emotional rollercoaster of trying to achieve pregnancy over and over again unless she has a deep-rooted desire to be a mother. I do not think my desire to be a mother will ever go away. My life is not everything that I wanted it to be, but I am working hard to make sure that it is everything it can be.

> My life is not everything that
> I wanted it to be, but I am working hard to
> make sure that it is everything it can be.

The age-old wisdom that time heals all wounds has been moderately true for me. I have noticed that each year gets easier to live with my childlessness. I have always dreaded October through December because of the triple threat: Halloween, Thanksgiving, and Christmas. This holiday season is filled with adorable children's costumes, school plays, Christmas morning presents, etc. This has always been the hardest part of the year for me.

I noticed that this year, it really was not that bad. I did not feel overly emotional. Of course, I have learned over the years not to allow myself to be around holiday parades, school plays, trick-or-treating, baby showers, baby dedications, or anything that will rip my heart out. Not participating in the things that trigger those feelings of sadness and loss has helped me feel much more grounded.

My close friend Chasity gave me a present this past Christmas that changed my outlook toward my remaining days on this planet. A card was included where she wrote about how she had kept walking past this plate in her dad's house and feeling like she should give it to me. The plate belonged to her dad; he had inherited it from his mother.

Chasity shared with her dad about her intense feelings surrounding this plate. Her dad was sweet enough to give Chasity the plate for me. Her card continued to say that she sincerely hoped that her gift did not upset me because she loved me and would never want to hurt me. After reading her card, I curiously opened the gift. When I saw the plate, tears poured down my cheeks. I was sitting next to my husband in the car at the time. We were on our way home from having dinner with Chasity and her husband. My husband kept asking me if I was okay. All I could say was "Thank You, God." I called Chasity to share this miraculous story.

Years ago, as I was walking through an antique store, I noticed a small German plate with a woman and the five children painted on it, along with the words Mors Dag 1972. I was born in 1972 in Wurzburg, Germany. Mors Dag means Mother's Day in German. The plate felt so personal for me, so I bought it and placed in my prayer closet. My husband did not even know I had the plate. So when I opened Chasity's gift and saw another copy of this plate, the thing she felt so strongly to give to me, I knew that God was letting me know my children are with Him. I knew in my spirit as I saw that second plate that I was not meant to be with my children in this life for whatever reason, but I would get to be their mother for eternity in heaven. It was so kind of God to allow me this peace. Each time I tell this story it makes me cry to remember how God can be so personal and sweet.

With God's help, I could have joy and purpose in this life as a childless mother. I think my children would want me to have joy and live my life to the fullest. This became my daily goal, and I have worked hard every day to meet it.

———•●•———

Chapter Four

My Rediscovery Model

I refused to stay in my misery, so this model was created after years of trying to find my way back to some type of joy. It took a long time and a lot of hard work, that quite frankly I did not have the energy. The determination to achieve this goal led me to read many books on communication, self-help, grief, and loss. I enrolled in several psychology courses at my local university and became a certified life coach. Many counselors helped me work through emotional triggers and marriage struggles.

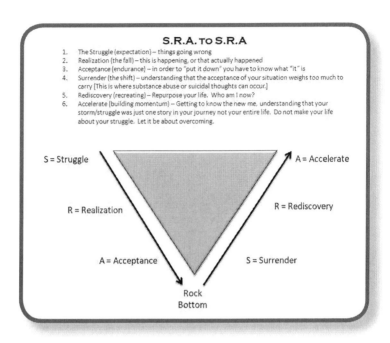

S.R.A. TO S.R.A

1. The Struggle (expectation) – things going wrong
2. Realization (the fall) – this is happening, or that actually happened
3. Acceptance (endurance) – in order to "put it down" you have to know what "it" is
4. Surrender (the shift) – understanding that the acceptance of your situation weighs too much to carry [This is where substance abuse or suicidal thoughts can occur.]
5. Rediscovery (recreating) – Repurpose your life. Who am I now?
6. Accelerate (building momentum) – Getting to know the new me, understanding that your storm/struggle was just one story in your journey not your entire life. Do not make your life about your struggle. Let it be about overcoming.

S = Struggle

A = Accelerate

R = Realization

R = Rediscovery

A = Acceptance

S = Surrender

Rock
Bottom

*I am not a grief expert only a veteran of it.
This model is an effort to gift you with
the map that helped me regain my joy.*

It will require many hours of your concentrated energy, but what other choice do you have? You can continue in your sadness and misery or discover the life in front of you. My hope is that you give the life in front of you a chance. It might surprise you. But, it is your choice to make.

This chapter shows you a basic outline of my Rediscovery Model. We will review each level in depth. It may appear that there is not much distinction between the levels, but while you are enduring heavy suffering progression between these levels can take years. I use my story to show you what I learned along the way and what caused setbacks. I have lived each level of my suffering, from gradual healing to eventual joy.

My Rediscovery Model is a tool for you to understand where you are in your healing process and how to work through and toward your next level.

Level One – *The Struggle*

This level directly pertains to the heart of your storm. This level feels as though you are surviving minute by minute in your daily life. Suffering comes in many forms: the death or separation of a loved one, the loss of a career, loneliness, divorce, trauma that involves physical and psychological lifestyle changes, or disease, to name just a few. There are so many tragic storms that people are forced to face in this life.

Some individuals do not realize they are suffering until it has cost them more than they have to give. They are struggling and forcing their way through life without stopping to understand the full effect of what has happened to them. This level involves the sole understanding that you are in a season of suffering.

**Think you've processed your pain?
Ask yourself these questions...**

- *What past experiences still rise up and cause you pain?*
- *Why do you think you keep revisiting this pain?*
- *Can you think of any part of your painful experience where you still need some healing?*

Level Two – *Realization*

This may seem like it should be obvious, but many people stay in denial for a while before realizing they are experiencing extreme emotional pain and suffering. Being able to simply admit to yourself what you are experiencing is a giant initial step in your healing process. This level deals with your acknowledgment of what has actually happened to you.

Level Three – *Acceptance*

After you realize that you have suffered a trauma or tragedy, understanding how that experience has changed you will take time. Acceptance is the awareness of how you and your life are different now, after your storm.

> **Do you think your current awareness of your life matches the reality of your life? If not, where do you think your disconnect might be?**

Level Four – *Surrender*

Level Four is where many people get stuck because you begin to see and accept the many differences in you and in your life. This level can be overwhelming. Spend some time here looking at what you need to release so that you can move forward.

> **What do you think keeps you from surrendering those things you cannot change?**

Level Five – *Rediscovery*

This is when you start to realize life could be good again and feel inspired to explore all of your options.

Level Six – *Accelerate*

Once you have decided to embrace your present life, you will learn to set and achieve new goals.

You have been introduced to a brief generalization of each level. The following chapters further reveal the healing that must take place through each level. Each chapter ends with questions to ask yourself to discover where you are in that process.

Chapter Five

The Struggle

Deep, unspeakable suffering may well
be called a baptism, a regeneration,
the initiation into a new state.

–GEORGE ELIOT

LEVEL ONE | THE STRUGGLE

*W*hen tragedy or trauma occurs in our lives, it can seem like time stands still. Our world seems unreal for a while. It takes time to realize what is going on. This feeling develops because the truth of what has transpired in your life is too painful to feel all at once. This is your brain's way of layering it out.

Our mind struggles as a result of our expectations not matching our reality. The life you have in your mind and heart is different than the life you are truly living. Your brain will replay your situation over and over again until you are able or willing to face your current reality.

Denial can be helpful until your heart and mind can agree on your reality. Denial is when you struggle with admitting to yourself the magnitude of the situation. It is an instinctual protective mechanism and it can last as long as you need it to. But, it is only meant to be temporary. Recovery from grief and tragedy take a lot of energy and hard work. The good news is that it is possible.

——————•●•——————

My Struggle

My expectation was to be able to stay pregnant and give birth to my baby. Thousands of women do it every day. My hope did not seem unreasonable. My struggle was watching my body miscarry over and over again. This had a ripple effect on every other area of my life. I had to go to battle for my sanity. My initial battle plan was just to keep moving and keep praying. That lasted for a while. I had experienced mood swings like depression and anger, along with body aches and pains from the hormones, procedures, and surgeries. I assumed that all of it was simply part of the infertility process, and that I needed to endure it and just move on. I found that I was not as resilient as I thought I was.

I experienced a lot of loss and grief over a short period. My heart was broken over the loss of my dog Mazzie to cancer and over the likelihood that I would never be a mother. I only had one heart, and each of these things was enough to break ten of my hearts. My days started to feel like I was swimming upstream in a muddy river. It took me a while to realize how depressed I was. Depression made me feel extremely tired. I could still function, but it took a great deal of effort. There were times when I would sit down on my sofa to rest for a minute and found myself there hours later without any concept of time.

I had known of several friends that had taken anti-depressants to combat their depression. I did not want to take any medications if possible. I had consumed enough chemicals, with all of the hormones added to my body over the past few years. I decided to try a holistic approach first. I researched foods that would help me combat depression (e.g., walnuts, leafy greens, avocados, seeds, beans, berries). I started going for walks and made myself get out of the house from time to time. I had always held the belief that I could heal myself with diet and exercise. I was wrong this time.

A few months after trying diet and exercise changes, I ended up calling my doctor for an anti-depressant. Two days into taking the meds, I felt like a cloud had lifted off of me and I could breathe again. It was such an amazing difference. I was back! Then it occurred to me that the prolonged years of sadness had chemically altered my brain. It troubled me to think about what I had put myself through over the past few years.

The psychologist I had been seeing gave me some wonderful advice during this time. She told me that in the same way I was able to change my brain with sadness, I could transform it back with laughter. Part of her homework for me was to find something that made me laugh every day. Thank you to the comedian Jimmy Fallon for Sara "Ew!" (Sara, without an h). Sara, along with a few other comedians, healed my brain.

I was able to get off of my anti-depressant after only a couple of months. My brain had to function correctly before I could properly heal. It would have been impossible for me to recover while I was depressed. I call depression "The Pause Button." It literally feels like you cannot function, everything just stops in you. The problem is that everything does not stop around you. The world keeps going.

Out of suffering have emerged the strongest souls; the most massive characters are seamed with scars.

−E. H. CHAPLIN

————— •●• —————

Your Struggle

Suffering in this life is unavoidable. Most suffering is brief, lasting only for a short season. Occasionally, the pain will stay for years or alter our lives forever. Some of us, like me, are unaware when we are entering a period of suffering. We are dangerous optimists. I kept telling myself "you're okay" over and over again. But, that was a lie I needed to believe to safeguard against the pain I was feeling. If you tend to smile and push on, like I did, then this level may take you a while.

Try to be honest with yourself about the expectations you had for life before the tragedy or trauma occurred. Be honest about how sad, disappointed, angry, or hurt you are. This part of the journey will require a lot of introspection. You may want to talk to a therapist and keep a journal to explore all of your emotions regarding your current situation. You must feel every part of this tragedy or trauma. There is not a way to cheat or escape these feelings. If you try to avoid your feelings, they have a tendency to pop up at times when you really do not want them to appear. Therapists refer to these as "triggers."

We all experience situations that "trigger" us during suffering. Over time, you will start to recognize the things or situations that elicit strong emotions. Pay attention to those things. Triggers are the areas of your heart that are wounded the deepest. If something triggers you, write down what happened to you or talk to your therapist

67

about it. Explore why it hurts so deeply. Acknowledging the severity of your pain will help you eventually heal from it.

You may have several triggers in the beginning of your healing journey, but they will minimize over time. In the beginning of my healing from infertility, every pregnant woman, every adorable baby, every happy family seemed to trigger me. I did not leave my house very often for this reason. Over time I have been able to be around these things more often without feeling depressed or envious. However, I had to make a conscious effort to work on my triggers. You will, too. They do not simply go away.

Try to explore some ways to work on your triggers. Art therapy was one that was helpful for me. One of my therapists had me place a drawing pad in my lap, close my eyes, then draw figure eights in all different directions for about a minute. When I stopped, she asked me to look at the image and color in the areas that stood out to me the most. This exercise brought up some complicated emotions for me. It allowed me to realize how much work I desperately needed to do to heal my broken heart.

There are many books on overcoming grief, recovering from trauma, self-help, divorce, etc. I recommend that you read as many as you can get in your hands. Even if you do not discover one that is specific to your situation, you can still find little things in each one of them that speak to you and help you heal.

———•●•———

God and Suffering...

Suffering is a difficult subject for most people, but can be very confusing for Christians. I wanted to address this to the best of my ability for you. I grew up in church and had heard many scriptures about how much God loved me. I prayed to God all the time and believed my prayers were often answered. When my husband and I were trying to have a baby, we had so many Christian friends and family praying over us. I knew God was with us, which was why it was so hard to fathom why God would keep allowing me to get pregnant only to miscarry over and over again.

Many well-meaning Christian friends encouraged us to confess our sins, as if our sinfulness prevented us from having a baby. It was not like we were living reckless lives. We were actually quite boring. One of my cousins informed me that she would need to pull away from me because my inability to stay pregnant after she had prayed so much had started to affect her faith in God. Many of these statements and opinions were too burdensome for me to handle in my current state of grief. I eventually realized that people were fallible, so I decided to focus on the word of God alone for answers.

I started to notice a pattern of suffering in every character in the Bible. Some of the most amazing characters, like Elisha, who had received double portions of the spirit of God (2 Kings 2:9) and who had participated in many of the most incredible miracles of the Old

Testament, spent his last days on this earth dying of a horrible disease (2 Kings 13:14).

John the Baptist jumped in his mother's womb when Mary visited while pregnant with his cousin Jesus (Luke 1:41). John the Baptist was kept holy and only allowed to eat locusts and honey (Matthew 3:4). The Bible says in Matthew 11:11, "Truly I tell you, among those born of women there has not risen anyone greater than John the Baptist." John the Baptist was beheaded after being imprisoned (Matthew 14).

All of Jesus' twelve disciples suffered tremendously. Peter was crucified upside down; Andrew was crucified; Thomas was killed by four soldiers with spears; Philip was put to death; Matthew was stabbed to death; Bartholomew was killed; James was stoned to death; Simon the Zealot was killed; and Matthias was burned to death. Paul wrote the majority of the New Testament, and he suffered with physical pain throughout his life (2 Cor. 12:7). Paul was beheaded. The entire story of Christ is centered on His suffering for the sins of all of mankind.

My point is that God never tells us anywhere in the Bible that we will not suffer in this life. As a matter of fact, he says the opposite. John 16:33 tells us that in this life we will have trouble, but Jesus tells us to "take heart" because He has overcome the world. God tells us in scripture that He has sent us a "Helper" and a "Comforter" called the Holy Spirit (John 14:26). He says in John 14:27, "Peace I leave with you; my peace I give to you. I do not give to you as the world gives. Do not let your hearts be troubled and do not be afraid."

Throughout my suffering, I did not see God changing my situation, but I did feel Him comforting me. He did help me along. I became curious why God wanted us to pray on all occasions (Eph. 6:18) when I felt like my prayers would not change my circumstances. I thought of it like a mom sitting her child on her lap and kissing their boo-boo for them after a fall. God was comforting me (like that mom) because he loved me, but I still was allowed to fall and scrape my knee. My prayers were allowing God to kiss my boo-boo's and spiritually love me during tough times.

It eventually occurred to me that God is focused on my holiness more than on my human experience. He uses many situations in life to draw me closer to Him. He tests me and requires my faithfulness in exchange for eternal salvation. His Holy Bible reads like the sweetest love story to me now. God moved through time and used so many lives to make His holy word eternal and to give all of us in this day and age the opportunity to know His love so intimately. Jesus Christ came with perseverance in His purpose to surrender His life as an eternal sacrifice so that God would see us through Christ and not in our sin. God sees us in Christ as a perfect and holy gift. God is not punishing us. God loves us dearly. He has given so much to allow us every chance to be with Him.

> ***God is focused on my holiness
> more than my human experience.***

We will all go through seasons of suffering. It will change us. But you can find joy again. You can heal, learn to adapt, and make other fulfilling relationships. It takes a lot of hard work and prayer. One day you will experience joy in your life once more, only this time, with a few more scars.

> ***Suffering has many stories, many
> faces. Each story is very personal.***

Outsiders...

Do not expect others to understand the depth of your suffering. How can they? They are not you. Is there that one person in your life who will let you lay your head in their lap and cry your eyes out, while they pet your hair without judgment? If so, you are blessed. Most of us do not have such a person. Hopefully, you do have at least one person in your life to talk with. Try not to share too much information with too many people. It is better to pick one or two people to trust. Hurting people require a lot of energy. Only the people who truly love you are going to be capable of giving you all of the strength you need.

You will know when you have shared too much, because someone will say something hurtful and ignorant to you. This happens to most of us. It is a good litmus test for realizing an over-share with the wrong person. Try to understand that those people simply do not yet know deep suffering. Be glad for them. You have been inducted into a club of knowing pain more deeply than you have ever known before. Once someone has endured great suffering, it is recognizable. There is a silent empathy those who have suffered share toward one another. You can see it in them.

———•●•———

Depression...

When suffering occurs in our lives, being sad is going to simply be part of it. Tragedy and trauma are extremely tough things to navigate. Working through emotions and coming to grips with unmet expectations will cause sadness. Suffering requires a lot of energy, so do not expect to be moving at top speed. Take time to rest and regain vital energy. It is essential to allow the body to rest and heal.

Depression is a strange animal that can slip up on you. If you suspect your brain chemistry is not functioning normally, talk to your doctor about it. Your doctor may recommend that you take an antidepressant to assist you in your healing. This is a very personal decision. The goal of the medication is to compensate for the brain's lack of these chemicals, over a period, until the brain is functioning normally again and the medication can be discontinued. This may take some experimentation in finding the proper drug and understanding when is the right time to wean off of the medication. It is crucial to work closely with your doctor while on any drug that alters your brain chemistry. You do not need any other obstacles during your period of healing.

1. Are you being honest with yourself about the level of pain you feel?

   _____

   _____

   _____

   _____

   _____

   _____

I did not allow myself to fully experience all of the pain I was collecting throughout my battle with infertility. I was afraid if I stopped to acknowledge it all, I would not be able to keep trying to get pregnant, and I desperately wanted to be a mother. I purposely blocked myself from feeling it all.

2. What is currently hurting your heart?

Try to write down what is hurting your heart in this very moment. If you can tap into a small vein of your pain, it can lead to the realization of your current reality. This is the start of Realization (level two).

3. Are you unable to sleep? What thought or feeling is waking you up or keeping you up?

I experienced repetitive fears and sadness that would keep me awake at night. Stress can be so exhausting that it can cause insomnia or loss of appetite. It is imperative that you try to get rest and proper nutrition. These two things are vital to keeping your energy level up while you work on healing your heart and mind.

Chapter Six

Realization

The only limit to our realization of
tomorrow will be our doubts of today.

- FRANKLIN D. ROOSEVELT

LEVEL TWO | REALIZATION

You have to be able to admit to yourself that your current circumstances are your truth. Realization happens when you can acknowledge, "This actually happened."

My Realization

My realization of my situation occurred in layers.

Layer One:

My faith was one of those layers. I had unwavering faith that God would answer our prayers and give us a baby. I was brought up to believe that God loved me deeply and listened to my prayers. We had all of our friends and family praying for us, plus people who had heard our story and were praying out of their compassion for our struggle. All of these people kept telling me that if I had faith in God, He would not let me down. I had heard story after story of how God had blessed so many other couples in their struggles to have a baby.

I am not sure when my hope turned into obsession, but it kept us trying to have a baby for way too long. One day it occurred to me that we had lost eleven babies and that number did not include the embryos that our embryologist discarded because they were not "Grade A" embryos. That realization made me fall into a pit of repentance. I questioned my sanity. I examined every choice we had made, even though we had prayed over each one of them. I wondered if I had been listening to God or making my own decisions.

Layer Two:

A couple of years after we had stopped trying to have children, my spirit had healed enough for me to awaken to the irreparable damage we had inflicted on our marriage. Some damage in marriage is like a piece of paper that has been crinkled up; you can flatten out the piece of paper again, but the wrinkles will always be there. Our marriage was full of wrinkles.

Layer Three:

We had not only put ourselves through tremendous grief and loss, but also our families and friends had been on the journey with us. It was hurtful to know that we had caused them so much pain as well. Some of my friends had stopped talking to me over the years. Our infertility journey had changed many of our relationships.

Layer Four:

One of the hardest changes for me to understand fully was how those years of infertility had changed my personality. I had been an outgoing, extraverted person who was always joking around and loved to laugh. My personality had changed to more of an introverted home-dweller who only wanted to be around people very infrequently. I was much more serious and carried sadness with me now.

———•••———

Your Realization

Realization occurs when you can admit what has happened to you. You are no longer in denial, the haze is clearing, and reality manifests itself. Realizing the truth usually comes in layers or waves over a period of time. This is the brain's way of protecting itself. You will get to a point when you can admit, "That really happened to me." Only then will you gain an understanding of what you have suffered.

Grief, loss, trauma, tragedy, and profound suffering can cause time to stand still. People have described this period of their lives as dream-like or surreal. When these surreal feelings start to sharpen, you get to a place where you are ready to admit to yourself what has happened in your life. The mind will have to say it over and over again until the heart believes it. This process takes time. Be generous in kindness with yourself. This is not the right time to be tough. This is part of the path to healing.

The toughest part of the realization process is admitting to yourself how you have been forever changed by what has happened. It is so sad to know you have lost a piece of yourself and to realize how you are now different. This is important work, because those closest to you will realize it before you do. It will be a future discussion to have with those who do life with you.

It is also excruciatingly painful to see how your decisions have affected the lives of the people you love. For example, a divorce will forever change your child's life, as well as the other extended relationships on either side of the family. This stage is only about realization, so pace yourself. The next layer will start to deal with Acceptance, where you will work through the many things that make up your present reality. For now, focus only on realizing what is happening in your suffering journey, in your heart and mind.

1. What has actually happened to you?

   _____

   _____

   _____

   _____

   _____

   _____

There was this one moment when all of a sudden, it occurred to me that I had lost eleven babies. If someone I knew had lost eleven babies over a three-year period, I would be shocked and so sad for them. I would also be concerned for any person suffering that much grief in such a short period of time. In my moment of realization, I was forced to break down the walls I had placed around that deep pain surrounding the loss of my babies. Those walls had protected me for long enough. In that moment, the pain was pushing through. It was time to realize the veracity of my feelings.

2. Name one or two people who are supporting you in your struggle. Why have you chosen these two people to support you?

_____

_____

_____

_____

_____

_____

In the middle of a crisis or tough season is not the ideal time to make friends. It is a very challenging time for your friends to know how to support you. It is kind of you to let those who are supporting you know what you need. Be cautious of your new supportive friend's intentions because if your drama is what attracted them to you, they may unintentionally try to keep you in it.

Chapter Seven

Acceptance

Accept what is, let go of what was
and have faith in what will be.

- UNKNOWN

LEVEL THREE | ACCEPTANCE

*T*hese levels get more and more difficult as you work
through them. Most would agree that **Level Four –
Surrender** is by far the most difficult. Accepting what
you have lost and how it has changed you must come
first. Acceptance comes in many layers. Your brain will
often give these layers to you in small pieces at a time. It
takes a while to realize and fully accept how tragedy or
trauma has influenced your life.

Even after you work through all of these levels, you may occasionally come back to **Acceptance** and **Surrender** as new layers of loss occur to you.

———•••———

My Acceptance

Assess the Damage...

Once I realized that my storm was over, I stood up, brushed myself off, and assessed the damage. This storm had changed me in many ways. Figuring out how I was different would be a part of my healing. I knew I would have to accept many things about myself that were hard to face.

Acceptance was an overwhelming process for me. Just using the word "overwhelming" does not even come close to how difficult this level was for me. I had so many complex emotions entangling the multiple losses I had experienced. I wondered if I had enough strength to accept everything I had lost. I knew I would never give birth or breastfeed my child, stare into the eyes of my baby as he or she lovingly stared back into mine, make pancakes for my family on Saturday mornings, or have those first days of school memories ... and on and on and on. There were lists and lists of things I knew that I would never get to experience. Having awareness of those things allowed me to start mourning them. I feared the many things I knew would come up that had not yet occurred to me.

My friends' Facebook posts became a good litmus test for how emotionally capable I was for dealing with the public most days. Being childless when you desperately want to be a mother and being stuck in a world full of beautiful families with lots of pregnant women everywhere is much like being an alcoholic trapped in a bar. There were some days when I knew I could not be in public without having an emotional breakdown. Crying in public is the worst.

RULE #4

Facebook is a good litmus test for the amount of personal crazy you may be carrying around with you. Your crazy is like a loaded gun.

People Are Not Perfect...

It was tough for anyone to understand how I was feeling during this time in my life. Plenty of well-intentioned people tried to comfort me by saying the most unbelievable and insensitive things. I prayed often to my heavenly Father that He would gift me with lots of grace for them and not let me say something hurtful that I might regret—or accidentally kill one of them. Something I continuously heard from those "helpful people" was that I should just relax and I would get pregnant. They would always couple their comment with a story of a friend who simply relaxed, stopped trying to get pregnant, then amazingly and immediately became pregnant and went on to deliver a healthy baby.

I could have been the most relaxed person in the world and would not have gotten pregnant without my fallopian tubes. Fallopian tubes are crucial in the pregnancy process. That comment would make me feel a little violent.

Another intrusive comment I regularly heard was that John and I should "just adopt." John was not open to adoption, so this comment usually brought up bad feelings for me. After our last attempt at in-vitro, John and I looked into the process of adoption. Unfortunately, we had endured several brutal years of infertility and the reality that adoption could bring more hardship into our lives was far too painful for my husband to even consider. He asked me if he was enough for me. Our marriage had not been a picnic up to that point, so I was not sure. Realizing that John was healing from years of grief and loss as well, I did not want to push the issue at that time. We shelved the conversation for about a year. That was about as long as I could stand not knowing if I ever had any chance of being a mother or not.

Unfortunately, after that year had passed, his answer was still no. I had wrestled with my empathy for my husband's concerns regarding adoption versus my desire to be a mother for several months before realizing my own feelings toward this situation. It was not my husband's fault we could not have children. He tried with me for years to have children and watched me suffer the loss of eleven babies. He told me once that he was not able to see me suffer the loss of a child ever again. We had heard so many stories about couples having to return the babies they had adopted to their biological families after the birth mother or father had changed their mind.

It was a heartbreaking conclusion, but I knew that we would not ever adopt. These are the layers of hurt and heartbreak people exposed every time they asked us, "Why don't you just adopt?" That question felt like a knife stabbing me in the gut. But how could any person have known all of the pain we had accumulated? This is why our ability to offer grace for those comments was always so essential.

I remember reading a quote that said, "Great suffering breeds great compassion." Those who have endured great suffering know never to try to make someone feel better with simple quotes or random stories. The most compassionate response to offer that person in the midst of their suffering is "I'm sorry."

Adding to My Acceptance List...

Over the past year, my husband and I started to make the transition from our friends with children still living at home to having more empty-nester friends. I was excited to think about finally getting a break from the constant conversations about children. But, we quickly realized that the conversation simply switched from children to grandchildren. I had been so overloaded by the many things I was missing out on by not being a mother. It had not occurred to me that I would never be a grandmother. I discovered an entirely new list of things that I would never get to experience in this life.

A friend of mine told me that the love of a grandchild is the sweetest love she has ever known. In that moment of feeling joy for my friend, I simultaneously felt tremendous pain in my heart in realizing I would never know the love she spoke of. My mind flooded with memories of fishing with my granddad while listening to his animated storytelling, and of playing Chinese checkers and sewing with my grandmother. My grandparents were such a wonderful part of my life. They seemed to truly enjoy us as we were growing up.

Children and grandchildren encompass the majority of joy a person gets to experience in this world. I was overwhelmed again with sadness thinking about all of the things I would never get to experience. I did not want to live as an unhappy person. I had to figure out how to stop being so sad all the time. I needed to discover other areas of life to find joy. But, I did not have a clue how to accomplish either task.

Personality Changes...

My husband and I found ourselves struggling in our relationship a couple of years after we had stopped trying to have children. We sat down with our pastor to gain new insight and a deeper perspective. In that meeting, our pastor asked my husband how I had changed throughout our marriage. My husband started to cry. I had seen my husband cry only a couple of times since I had known him. It broke my heart.

I had been unaware that the grief and loss I had experienced over the years had changed my personality. My personality was the last thing on my mind. But, it had started to affect my marriage, so I had to pay attention to it. I asked my husband how I was different. He explained that I had become a much more serious person, quieter, more subdued, and isolated. It made him sad to see me like that.

I had always been an extravert with lots of friends. Through the years of infertility, I had lost several of those friends. It was very hurtful when my friends stopped taking my calls and disappeared from my life. Some people are not good at being long-term encouragers.

I did not have the energy to meet new friends. Staying away from others was simply easier for me at the time. Isolation was necessary for a season, but it had begun to take the life out of me, like a wild animal that had been caged for too long.

Spirituality Changes...

I was raised in the Christian church, where I learned about Jesus and His love for me. Our family held hands to pray over every meal, and we prayed each night before we went to bed. Our large family would gather at my grandparents' house for lunch after church every Sunday. All of us grandchildren would be playing games on the living room floor while the women were cleaning the kitchen and the men were discussing the pastor's sermon.

My granddad is the patriarch of the family and is very knowledgeable about the word of God. Some of my best memories as a child were listening to my granddad, my dad, and my uncles discuss scripture on those Sunday afternoons.

I was ten years old when my parents divorced. My mom and I ended up living across town. My dad was laid off and had to move out of state to find employment. Our lifestyles changed drastically. My mom turned to alcohol and seemed to lose herself for a few years after the divorce.

My dad's family, as well as our church family, disowned my mom. All of the sudden, many of the people I had grown up with simply went away. This was hard for me to understand. We were all dealing with the loss of our family in different ways. We stopped attending church. My mom was bitter toward the church because they were so hateful to her after the divorce.

The subject of God seemed to fall away as well. I would still talk to God, but the experience through these years of my life kept me away from church for many years. It was not until I was thirty-four years old when I joined a church again. That span of time between ten years old and thirty-four years old was filled with insecurity, destructive fun, dysfunction, alcohol abuse, sexual promiscuity, and lots of wild and crazy stories. I rarely made wise decisions for myself during these years. It would take another book or two to write about this time in my life. By the grace of God, I feel like I did alright for a young person who had pretty much raised herself.

My childhood church body may have left me, but I knew God was always with me. I could feel Him and see Him in my life. I remember times when I would be drinking during high school parties and felt the conviction of God in my spirit. In my small little country town, many of the teenagers would race cars and drink beer for entertainment. There was not much else to do.

Once when I was doing both, I almost wrecked my 1965 Mustang. It would have been a bad wreck. Supernatural interference was the only way I could explain not wrecking. I knew my guardian angels were with me throughout those years of my life. They had shown up for me several times. This was so confusing to me. I thought that you had to go to church, read your Bible, and pray all of the time for God to love you. I was not doing any of that, but I still felt His love for me.

All of my life other people told me who God was, but their definition versus who He was now showing me He was were very different. Out of curiosity, I started to read the Bible for myself. I wanted to know more about the character of God. I prayed and asked God to remove any untruths from my heart and mind, and to replace them with His truth. It was the beginning of an incredible journey.

Over the next several months, God started to separate me from the things that were interfering with my spiritual growth. One example of what He did was to open my eyes to my artwork. Apparently, every piece of art I had collected over the years had naked people in them. Not that there is anything wrong with naked people, but my art was a bit erotic. The interesting thing was that I never really noticed. Or perhaps, I was so conditioned to another way of life that I just didn't see it.

Another example was when God had me clean out my DVD collection. I am a big movie buff and loved violent action films. All of my Quentin Tarantino movies had to go. I also chose to stop drinking alcohol. Many of my most painful memories involved the use of alcohol. I needed to cleanse my life from the things that were blinding me to God's goodness.

All of these changes were necessary to shed away who I was for long enough to become who He wanted me to be. The funny thing was that once I grew in knowledge and faith, God didn't care what I chose to watch or how I decorated my house. He needed me to mature spiritually so that my desires would change.

My artwork is different now, but I do have a nude bust of myself that my cousin made for me in my guest bathroom. I also own Quentin Tarantino's movie True Romance again, but I turn off the crude language when I watch it. And, my husband and I have an occasional glass of wine. My spiritual training wheels have been taken off.

There is a scripture in the Gospel of John that reads, "My sheep listen to my voice; I know them and they follow me. I give them eternal life and they shall never perish; no one can snatch them out of my hand. My Father, who has given them to me, is greater than all; no one can snatch them out of my Father's hand. I and the Father are one." These words were so reassuring to the young girl of my heart, who had felt abandoned by her church and much of her family at a young age.

Jesus would never leave me; His Father (God) who is the creator of all things would never allow it. How wonderful. I spent two years studying, worshiping, and praying to mature my faith. I felt that God was with me every second of my day. He made me laugh, dance, cry, and think deeply about many things. This time for me was essential spiritual nourishment. It prepared me for the battle I was about to face.

When I met and married my husband, my relationship with God changed. My focus was on my marriage. I was spending so much time with my husband that I was not worshiping or praying as much, but my relationship with God was anchored in His truth and forever sacred to me. It was not too long after this time that my faith was tested.

When I realized I was miscarrying for the second time, I fell on my knees in uncontrollable tears begging God to not take my baby. I had shameful guilt knowing that my faith was so small. I felt God's comfort with me over the next several days during that miscarriage. That experience confused me. I wondered why God would allow me to go through such pain if He loved me so much. There was something in all of it that I was missing.

I went on to become pregnant three more times and lost all three babies. Over time, I stopped praying and reading my Bible. I had begun to believe that I was being punished. I was worried that I had done something to upset God. Logically, I knew God did not work that way. Unfortunately, my feelings were dominating my heart during this time in my life.

I would have conversations with God in my head, but never in deliberate prayer time. My spiritual relationship had really taken a hit from all of the loss I had experienced over such a short period of time. All my doubts and questions consumed me until I eventually avoided anything spiritual. I was spiritually fickle in my relationship with God, but not in my belief of Him.

Anytime I tried to talk with my friends about these feelings, they would just say something really churchy, which frustrated me and made me angry. I once confided in my pastor about my feelings, explaining to him my inability to read my Bible or pray. He recommended to me a book on spiritual maturity. It was so disappointing and only made me feel more isolated and alone in my battle. So, I stopped talking to people about it. I decided I was alone in my suffering.

RULE #5

*Do not be legalistic
with hurting people.*

One day while I was crying to God about feeling like the only woman on this planet who was childless, God led me to my Bible. He had me open to Genesis 11:30, where I read that Abraham's wife Sara had lived eighty-three years as a barren woman; Genesis 25:21 said that Isaac's wife Rebekah was barren; Genesis 29:31 said that Jacob's wife Rachel was barren. First Samuel told a story about a woman named Hannah who suffered with childlessness. Hannah cried so hard and loud in that story that a priest named Eli thought she was drunk.

God showed me that women had been suffering with childlessness since the beginning of mankind. This was strangely comforting to me. I had felt so alone in my childlessness. God was showing me that I was one of many women who had to endure childlessness. Simply knowing I was not alone helped me, but my heart was still broken. Every woman around me seemed to get pregnant every time her husband touched her.

I knew how much God loved me, but I questioned why He would allow me to go through this. I found myself questioning the meaning of my life and wondering what my purpose in this life might be. This was a very difficult time for me spiritually. I seemed to vacillate between times of begging God to help me through the pain and times when I tried very hard to block the thought of Him out completely.

Over time, I began to pray more and allow God to help me through my grief. Instead of blocking Him out, I started trying to block out all of the many painful questions reeling through my mind. I knew many of those questions would never have answers and would only keep me in pain. Stopping the unanswerable questions was incredibly hard for me. It had become such a bad habit—an addiction. I needed it to stop. Eventually, with God's help, it did.

RULE #6

*God is a good Father
who loves you.*

*Never stop praying to Him,
even when it's hard.*

Ritual and Ceremony...

I remembered reading a story several years ago about the Tana Toraja people of the mountainous region in southern Indonesia. The villagers buried their stillborn babies in hollowed-out spaces in the trunks of trees, then would cover them with mud and straw. The villagers believed the baby's life joined with, and continued in life within, the tree.

The villager's story came to my mind when I was contemplating the type of ceremony I could have for my babies. Ceremony and rituals allow people celebration, honoring, and remembrance. I knew I needed to do something to honor my babies' lives. The first thing I needed to do was to give them all names. I wrote them a letter telling them all of the things I wish we had gotten to experience together, then I burned the letter and I said a prayer surrendering them to the hands of God. I designated the last week of the year to honor and mourn their lives.

December was the month when our second IVF failed in ectopic pregnancy. This month symbolizes the most difficult time of our infertility years for me. It is also after the Christmas holiday, which is such a heartbreaking time of year to be childless. If I allowed myself to mourn the months of each loss, I would be mourning six months out of the year. I allow myself this one week to cry and be sad, and then the hope of a brand New Year begins.

Getting Out There...

Halloween is one of the biggest kid holidays that my husband and I celebrate. This holiday dominates a great many of my mom fantasies. I wanted to make costumes and take my kiddos out trick-or-treating so bad. Because of my childlessness, I would lock myself in my house and uninstall Facebook to keep me from seeing all of the adorable families enjoying what I would never get to enjoy.

I would occasionally bake cookies or make popcorn balls during the Halloween season, or some little treat for my husband and I to enjoy. But, I really wanted to be doing these things with our children. My husband and I did not even eat sweets. I would force my husband to let me paint our faces, dress us up in costumes, then drag him out to an adult Halloween party. It was a way for me to focus on something other than the unbearable sadness that filled my heart.

This year, I did not need to uninstall Facebook or celebrate the holiday in any way. It has been four years since we have stopped trying to have children. I guess that is how long it has taken me to deal with some of my triggers. I know it sounds strange, but it concerned me that I was not sad. Do not misunderstand me. I am pleased that the endless images of adorable children and family events did not leave me in a pile of soggy Kleenex this year. But that sadness has shielded me for so long. It gave me an excuse to shelter myself.

Now that I am getting stronger, it feels a little scary to get out there and start participating in social events. Honestly, just because it does not devastate me does not necessarily mean I want to rub my nose in it. Maybe some year it will just be another holiday. This child-filled world can still be a little too much for my heart from time to time.

———————•●•———————

Your Acceptance

After the realization of what has occurred in your life, explore everything that was lost because of it. How did this tragedy or trauma change your personality, relationships, and spirituality? Has it affected your physical health, job/career, or the ability to take care of yourself? Now that the storm has passed, you will need to access the damage. This level may take a while. The brain will only give this information in layers. It is emotionally draining to take an inventory after a storm.

This level requires a lot of introspection and awareness. It takes a while to grasp the thousands of things about your present and future that have been affected. This can be a very daunting and depressing thing to do. If you do not already have a journal and therapist, you will definitely need one for this level. It would not be a bad idea to have a good friend or two to have available during this level as well. The difficulty in this level revolves around admitting what it took from you, all the fantasies and expectations you had about your life that you are mourning.

1. Make a list all of the ways your life is different now.

    _____

    _____

    _____

    _____

    _____

    _____

At this point in your journey, you may want to purchase a journal. Acknowledging your complete and total loss is a process and happens gradually over time. Your ability to acknowledge the loss allows you the opportunity to grieve it.

2. How will these changes affect your life?

    _____

    _____

    _____

    _____

    _____

    _____

Loss and grief change us. Once you start to understand how you are different, you can begin to find yourself again.

3. Do you see your need for a counselor and/or support group?

    _____

    _____

    _____

    _____

    _____

    _____

There are times in our lives when the suffering has been too much for us to handle. Sometimes we need others to help us heal. There are wonderful people equipped to do that very thing. Finding them is your task. I have had several counselors really help me.

Finding the right support is a personal preference and is a little like dating. If you are going to be vulnerable and bear your heart, then you want that person to be compassionate, empathetic, and a good listener, and to ask thoughtful questions that create intentional thinking for you during your conversations. Ask for a reference from trusted sources and make sure you meet with the counselor or support group to ask questions about their plan to help you before you jump in.

You will have a limited amount of energy after your season of suffering, and it is crucial that you proceed with caution. Some people take more energy than they give. Surround yourself with people who fuel your energy.

———•●•———

Chapter Eight

Surrender

Transformation begins on the
other side of surrender.

- U N K N O W N

LEVEL FOUR | SURRENDER

Surrender happens out of necessity. Once you start the process of Acceptance, the many layers of things you have lost begin to feel overwhelming in your heart. The weight will eventually become unbearable. Many people will need to use coping mechanisms to endure this process. Some examples of positive coping mechanisms are faith and prayer, exercise, and journaling. Examples of negative coping mechanisms include alcohol and drug abuse. This is also the level when some will contemplate suicide.

———•••———

My Surrender

Untangling...

Many of the Christian self-help books I had read suggested that I could simply lay my worries down at the feet of God. For me, true surrender was not letting God have control in a place where I had none. God had been with me the entire time. He was already in control of everything. My problem was not in recognizing *what* I needed to surrender. My problem was in understanding *how* to surrender it. That entire process was very confusing for me.

RULE #7

Internal battles are never won alone.

My pain was so intertwined with my identity as a mother. Surrendering any of it felt like I had to surrender the memory of my babies, and that if I moved on with my life and allowed myself to be happy I would be dishonoring the loss of them.

My miscarriages were strange deaths for me to process. These were my babies who lived their entire lives inside of my body. No one had held them, kissed their lips, or seen their sweet faces. I knew people would forget about them very quickly. But as their mother, I could never forget about them. I clutched to their existence and the fantasy of their lives so they would not disappear. They deserved to be remembered. They mattered.

I wrestled with how to surrender their loss and still hold on to them. In time, I realized that it was impossible to do both. I had to figure out how to honor their lives and let them go. There were so many fantasies I had created in my mind that I would need to release. When I would see another mother enjoying her children, I would fantasize about getting to do all of those things with my children. I did this often. Those fantasies were addictive. Unfortunately, they always ended in disappointment, tears, and chocolate. Once the fantasy had played out, my reality would sink back in. I would never be a mother.

That statement ... ouch!

Surreal World...

I found myself staying home as much as possible. The world was full of moms, happy pregnant women, and so many adorable little kiddos. It was so painful to leave my house. I would get out from time to time, put on a smile, and socialize. Everyone would ask me how I was doing and I would lie. People did not want to listen to the truth, and I did not want to hear myself say it. It took an enormous amount of energy to fake being alright. On the inside, I was a wreck and had no clue as to how I would even begin to move on.

In my mind was a fantasy of a family that would never happen. I found myself so weighed down by sorrow that I struggled to pry myself off the couch for days on end.

Whispers...

I knew that if I could not find a way to surrender my sadness, it would kill me. I truly did not understand how to do that. I began praying about it, asking God to help me. That was when the whispers started. The whispers would tell me that I had no future, I was going to die alone with no children to care for me, society would not see me as a woman now, and I should just kill myself to spare myself a lifetime of loneliness and pain.

RULE #8

Physical pain is a sign of something wrong.

Emotional pain works the same way.

The whispers reminded me that I had many bottles of pain medications left-over from all of my surgeries. Each day the whispers got louder and more frequent. I did not think I was suicidal, but it consumed more of my thoughts than I was comfortable with, so I decided to talk to a counselor.

RULE #9

Everyone contemplates suicide once or twice in life, BUT if you start working out in your mind how you are going to do it you should tell someone immediately.

Counselors...

Finding the right counselor was not as easy as I thought it would be. My first counselor was horrible. For sixty full minutes, he listened to me complain about my life, my discontentment, my marriage troubles, and my feelings of loneliness. At the end of our first session, he advised me to leave my husband. I left his office so angry and confused. My husband and I had a strained marriage, and his recommendation left me contemplating leaving my husband.

A friend of mine told me, "Hurting people hurt people." People who are suffering are self-centered. That self-focus is required to survive the pain they feel. Self-centered people struggle in their relationships. I read a statistic once that said 90% of couples that experience the loss of a child end in divorce within a year. My husband and I were hurting from all of the grief and loss we had suffered, but I simply could not fathom losing my husband too.

The second counselor I went to showed me an amazing tool that I still use to this day. She taught me how to run fear to its end. I had many fears about my life. She would take each fear statement I made and ask me, "And then what would happen?" Once I would answer, she would ask me the same question. That exercise made me realize that even if all of my fears had actually happened, I would eventually be okay. Although that was a helpful exercise to tackle my fears, my grief and loss were still overwhelming me. Just talking to her about my life was not enough. I needed a counselor to walk me through healing.

I then sought out a counselor with some knowledge in the world of infertility. I found a woman about my age who had also endured infertility. This counselor asked me to keep a Pinterest board of all the pictures that fed my fantasies of motherhood. That exercise turned into a heart-wrenching addiction. I tried that for weeks, only to find myself feeling worse, not better. I could not stay in that space of constant sadness any longer. I decided to stop seeing her.

Up until this moment, I didn't think my issues were serious enough for a psychologist. I had a common misbelief that counselors were for people with difficult life issues, but psychologists helped those who had more serious psychological disorders. After becoming so frustrated with the counselors I had seen, I decided to see a psychologist in hopes that I would finally get the help I desperately needed.

I found a local Christian psychologist, Melissa, who ended up being my Goldilocks therapist—she was just right. She listened to me tell her about my previous counselors and what I needed from her. She told me to delete my Pinterest Board of mothering fantasies. She explained that this type of activity was for people who had not yet realized their loss and that this exercise was preventing me from moving on.

Melissa patiently listened to the rest of my crazy story and then said to me, "I'm impressed that you're sane." We both laughed. I knew she was trying to be funny, but that meant something to me coming from a psychologist. There were so many times I had felt insane. From that moment on, her comment became my mental Purple Heart award.

Melissa worked with me on my past as well as my future. Our discussions about my future allowed me to hope again. She helped me understand that my life still had purpose, even if I would never be a mother. We continued meeting over the next several months, until one day she told me that there was no need for me to return. She felt like I was ready for the next chapter of my life and that I should go live it.

When I left her office that day, I sat in my car for a while before leaving the parking lot as that sentence echoed in my mind: "I feel like you are ready for the next chapter of your life, and you should go live it."

Moving On...

Melissa's statement gave me permission to move on. I could move on. It also scared the hell out of me. At that moment, I realized that choosing not to move on would be choosing to live in discontentment. Discontentment did not sound like the future I was wanting. I knew I had to press forward; I just did not know what I was moving toward. All of my previous fantasies about my life had included children. I had to come up with all-new fantasies.

There are no models for childless living. I could not think of any individuals who lived a full life without children. What do people without children do? I thought of a few celebrities who never got pregnant, but remembered that they all had recently adopted. The only person on the planet I could think of was Dolly Parton. I recalled reading an article about how she could not have her own children and suffered from depression because of her childlessness throughout her life. I thought if Dolly could figure out a way to live her life to the fullest, then so could I.

———•●•———

Your Surrender

I do not believe true surrender can occur without God. Healing from deep pain is supernatural. Knowing you need to surrender your pain is easy to acknowledge. Understanding how to surrender that pain is impossible until you realize that only God can do what you cannot.

I do not believe true surrender can occur without God.

Surrender occurs out of necessity. Once you start compiling your list of things at the Acceptance level, you will need to be able to surrender all of it. The process of surrendering is tough because you will feel yourself wanting to hang on to every little fantasy you had about your life. This is the level I refer to as "rock bottom." You will either hold on to your pain or you will surrender it. The choice is yours to make.

This level is the reason I wrote this book. I almost got lost. Eventually, I was able to surrender my pain and disappointment. I see so many people get stuck at this level. This is the level where healthy coping mechanisms (like prayer and journaling) or unhealthy coping mechanisms (like alcohol or drugs) become a part of your lifestyle, or maybe a bit of both.

You can choose to live in anger and discontentment. I have witnessed plenty of people who have made this blatant decision and who stop in their healing process and live in this place of heart-numbing bitterness.

This is the level where suicide may come to mind. Most flirt with the thoughts of ending their pain, but if you find that you are starting to plan it out, it's imperative to talk to someone about it. It can be hard to fight all of those negative whispers when you are so tired and low on energy. This is why it is so necessary to surround yourself with people who can lift you up. There are so many resources available to encourage you. Find them!

I read a very tragic book written by Joan Didion called *A Year of Magical Thinking* during this time in my life. Joan made me feel like I was not the only person in this world who had experience intense loss and pain. Although our loss was different, I felt a sisterhood with her.

I also listened to some online sermons from biblical teachers who encouraged me, like Craig Groeschel, Mike Fabarez, Patricia Shirer, and Joyce Meyer, just to name a few. I knew I needed to surrender all of my pain, but I did not know how to do it. It required daily prayer, asking God for help. I truly believe surrender is impossible without the help of God. It has to be supernatural. I do not think it is humanly possible.

Early churches created labyrinths for this purpose. The labyrinth has a winding path to its center, where there is a prayer bench. You were supposed to walk the winding path to the bench, where you stopped to lay all of your worries at the feet of God. The bench is the place to surrender all. The second half of the labyrinth's winding path symbolizes moving away from your worries and leaving them behind with God. This is a beautiful ritual to experience, and most cities have a labyrinth available to the public. There are many different kinds of rituals that can be helpful in the healing process.

One of my practices included writing a letter to the babies I had miscarried, saying a prayer over them, and then burning the letter. This was symbolic of me surrendering them to the hands of God. I understand that although I cannot experience my children in this life, I will be with my children in heaven throughout eternity. I remember reading where someone had described it as having real estate in heaven. Rituals are very personal, and they are meant to help you surrender the unbelievable pain you have endured.

———•••———

Do not attach the love for the person you lost to your pain. Do not anchor yourself to the pain to validate the loss. Pain is the result. It is not the person you loved. You do not have to carry pain as a badge of honor. Moving on is not forgetting. Surrendering is not forgetting. You simply choose to no longer carry it around like luggage.

———•••———

1. What are your coping mechanisms?

———————————————————————————————————
———————————————————————————————————
———————————————————————————————————
———————————————————————————————————
———————————————————————————————————
———————————————————————————————————

I read several statistics on childless women becoming alcoholics after their battle with infertility. I was careful not to allow myself to fall down that rabbit hole. If you know you are inclined to be drawn toward a negative coping mechanism, talk to someone about it. You will need serious accountability during this time in your life. I call negative coping mechanisms "lazy fixes." Positive coping mechanisms may be more challenging for you and require stamina. It can be hard to stir up that extra energy at times, but the results are going to be so much better and your healing time shorter.

2. Do you have an accountability person checking in with you?

_____

_____

_____

_____

_____

_____

I hope that you have someone whom you allow to hold you accountable in your life. If you have not done this yet, let me encourage you to invite a person you trust to speak blunt truth to you. This is a hard relationship, but is so necessary for your healing. A person who provides accountability for you will help you to keep your personal boundaries, respect your body and values, and lead you to thoughtful decision making.

Chapter Nine
Rediscovery

To achieve your potential,
you'll have to rediscover the joy.

−AMANDA BORDEN,
OLYMPIC ATHLETE

LEVEL FIVE | REDISCOVERY

Rediscovery only occurs after you choose to move forward despite your loss. You could choose to live in discontentment. Many people have never moved past their tragedies or traumas. They stay mad at "life" or "God" and grow in their bitterness. This doesn't have to be your outcome. Ultimately, the choice is yours.

Note for the skeptic:

Let me say something to those who are reading this and mentally cussing me right now, because you believe that your current mindset is not a choice for you. If there is some tiny part of your heart that wishes to live differently than you are living, I would ask that you give this book a chance. I too almost got lost in bitterness, sadness, and discontentment. When you run out of energy from all of the pain in your heart, sometimes you pause to take a break then never move forward again. Misery can be strangely comfortable. But my friend, you were meant for so much more! Pray, ask someone (or several) for help, get some counseling, go to group therapy. You will probably have setbacks, but keep trying. Take it an hour at a time until you make it to a day at time.

Once you choose Rediscovery, you have the challenging task of figuring out who you are now—now that you are different. You will obviously need to get to know the new you to figure out how to move forward. Many of these levels take time, probably years. The healing of your heart and mind is a lengthy and necessary process. These steps require a great deal of work, but not as much as discontentment and bitterness.

My Rediscovery

There was something noticeable behind the eyes of those who had endured great suffering, as if we were all now a part of some sort of spiritual kinship. I understood now that all suffering is part of the same storm that we will all experience in this lifetime. My awareness produced a deep compassion in me for others, for those who had experienced the storm, as well as for those who had no idea what was going to happen to them.

Here's the Truth...

I know now that I am not alone. God did not take me aside and punish me. Life did not turn its back on me. I am simply in a world where there is suffering. I am no different than anyone else on the planet. My present understanding of suffering made me cling to joy even more tightly. I never realized how important it was to laugh, tell fun stories, and live in kindness with others.

Gathering Tools...

My new outlook on life made me want to gather as many tools as I could for surviving those seasons of suffering. I thought if I could collect several helpful tools, I could bless others by sharing what I had learned. This hunt started at my local university. I enrolled in a bunch of psychology classes. Psychologists have been studying human behavior for decades. I was sure that I could gather some tools there. My favorite courses were "Motivation & Emotion" and "Death, Dying & Bereavement."

"Motivation & Emotion" taught me about Abraham Maslow and William Glasser's description of every person's essential needs in this life. I learned the difference between something we need and something we want. Needs are for our essential well-being, whereas wants are things we yearn for. I *need* a house to live in, and a job to earn money and contribute to society. I *want* a nice home, an awesome career, an abundance of money, and love from my community. The difference in these two examples is motivation.

As I began to study motivation, I started to understand that each person has a unique perspective on everything. Understanding a person's perception is key to motivating them. One has to be trained in listening to verbal and non-verbal communication. This was when I began researching the art of listening, which led me to life coaching. A significant portion of my life coach training was on the art of listening, hearing the things people were not saying, and helping them to say it. Creating that awareness allowed for further growth.

———— •◦• ————

Your Rediscovery

Once the choice has been made to try to move out of the pain, you are ready for Rediscovery. I call this level Rediscovery because you are different after a season of suffering. You may have an entirely new perspective on life, or different priorities in life. However, your trauma or tragedy has changed you. Rediscovery is the fun and challenging process of getting to know this new you. Rediscovering this new life feels hopeful. You start to feel the sunshine on your face again. You realize that you have survived the storm and begin making plans for this newly seen future.

Remember that the storm may have taken up a few chapters of your life, but it is not your entire book. You may choose to use your tragedy to help others, as I am doing with this book and with my life coaching. But, I want to encourage you to find other things, outside of serving others, that will bring joy to your heart. I also enjoy gardening, painting, beading, and taking my dogs for long walks on our acreage. Serving others is wonderful work, but you are still healing. People consume energy, so you will need to nurture your spirit and allow time for rest.

There are a few times in life when we need a team of people to help us get through our current situation. For example, when you go through a divorce, a lawyer is required, as well as a financial advisor, a counselor, and perhaps a realtor. I encourage you to seek out a team of people who can assist you in every level of the healing process. Do not be afraid to fire people and move on when it is not a good fit. I went through about six counselors until I found the right one for me. Do not settle if it is not a good fit.

When you get to a place where you are ready for Rediscovery, consider adding a life coach to your team. Life coaches are trained to pay close attention to your body language, cadence, and tone and will ask you deep-thinking questions to help you navigate this phase of your healing. Life coaches are people who are passionate about helping individuals live a life they love. As a life coach, I have worked on teams with counselors, psychologists, and pastors to help individuals heal from tragedy, trauma, grief, and loss.

1. Why have you chosen to move past your circumstances, trauma, or tragedy?

   _____

   _____

   _____

   _____

   _____

   _____

Living in your present can be extremely difficult, especially if your tragedy involved the loss of someone you love. It may be easier knowing that although God has reunited with their soul, He has graciously allowed you to keep all of the love they have given you over the years. Learning how to carry their love without their physical presence is the task before you. This is why one day's difficulties are enough to navigate. An intense season of suffering increases your awareness that life is incredibly precious. Train your mind to live in the present moment. Do not let suffering block out the things that are good in your life.

2. What have you learned about yourself through this season of suffering?

_____

_____

_____

_____

_____

_____

I learned that I was a dangerous optimist. My optimistic hope in the process of IVF became a poison for me. I should have stopped trying to have a baby long before I did. It is always easier to see our mistakes in retrospect. Now that I know that I can be overly optimistic, I will usually ask my accountability partner or husband to weigh in on my decisions.

3. How have your grown in knowledge and perseverance throughout this season of your life?

_____

_____

_____

_____

_____

_____

Suffering is powerfully molding to our spirits. It quickens us to a perception we never knew previously. After my season of suffering I could easily see pain in others, even through masks and fake smiles. It was something in their eyes. Suffering changed me like the beating of iron—it made me sharper in a lot of ways.

4. What will you do when you have a setback?

_____

_____

_____

_____

_____

_____

You will have setbacks. Give yourself permission to be sad, angry, or whatever you feel. Let yourself cry or yell. Get it out, and then go wash your face and carry on.

The pain you went through was life-altering. Pain can lie dormant in your body for a period of time, but can flare up occasionally. It may take time to work through. This is normal and should be expected. By this time in your healing process, you have begun to understand how to care for yourself when experiencing setbacks.

———•●•———

Chapter Ten

Accelerate

Nothing great was ever achieved
without enthusiasm.

– EMERSON

LEVEL SIX | ACCELERATE

*Y*ou have survived the storm. You have emerged a new person, now different than before. Your Rediscovery process has helped you to identity the new you and how you have changed. The Acceleration process requires self-encouragement to keep your momentum going in the right direction. It is easy to have setbacks after tragedies and traumas.

Like I mentioned previously, you may occasionally need to go back to Acceptance and Surrender levels as new layers of loss are realized. Always look for ways to Accelerate your new life. Accelerating a new path requires you to remain in the present moment. It is a constant exercise of making today the best day it can be.

I know the inner strength, time, and energy it takes to move through all of these levels. Please know that it took me years to work through my pain and sadness. I had many setbacks, but knew I could not stay in my misery. Keep working through each level. You will get there.

———————•●•———————

My Acceleration

The losses I endured were only one part of my story. The grief had changed many different areas of my life. It was important to me that I not let this chapter in my life become the end of my story. Multiple disappointments had wrapped themselves around my heart, but I was determined to persevere. Around the time I began to feel I was going to be okay, I felt called to write this book. My suffering created a passion in me to coach others in their rediscovery and provide tools that could help their lives be somewhat easier through their suffering journey.

Life Coaching...

My suffering journey almost cost me my marriage. In my effort to heal our relationship, I read many books on communication and how to have a better marriage. I took several psychology courses at my local university and became a life coach. I needed tools to renew our commitment and intimacy. Because of the marriage difficulties I had faced during many tough times, I gained passion and empathy for couples who were also struggling.

I was familiar with the constant heartbreak of a strained marriage. I had begun to see the mistakes we all make in our communication, with passive-aggressive behavior, as well as faking it and all of the other silly things we all do when we do not know what to do. Many married couples become trapped by unhealthy habits. I wanted to provide others with the useful tools and skills I had learned from all of the teachers and authors who had generously shared their mistakes and knowledge with me.

I spent several months writing a relationship communication coaching course loaded with powerful relationship-building tools. These areas included how to develop discernment, clearly creating and enforcing boundaries, understanding needs, and recognizing unspoken and unrealistic expectations. I also described destructive communication habits to avoid, while teaching several useful communication tools for any relationship. I included a section to encourage others to work toward continually strengthening their relationships, while providing suggestions on how to invest in their relationships that ensures positive momentum.

The last section of the course included a workbook with a question and answer section to help participants discern what they were contributing to their relationship and to create awareness in areas where they can make improvements. I did my best to help my clients grasp that all communication starts in your heart and mind first before it is taken to your spouse. Introspection is always a healthy first step in communication. My relationship communication coaching course was beneficial to several couples. This made my heart happy.

Your Acceleration

Once you find a purpose beyond your pain, it is essential to keep that forward momentum. I understand that grief never really disappears. This can cause setbacks that will take you back into the levels of having to Accept and Surrender. When this happens, do not camp out there. Do the work and get back to your life at present. This level is a constant exercise of making today the best day it can be.

Everyone loves stories of perseverance. There are so many great stories available these days of individuals who have overcome their circumstances. I watch motivational videos all the time. I have a collection of them. They have fed my spirit and helped me push myself to fight for joy and health. When my body feels good, it makes it easier for my mind to cooperate, which brings joy to my soul.

RULE #10

Your story matters.

1. How will you use what you have learned for continual personal growth?

   _____

   _____

   _____

   _____

   _____

   _____

Good warriors will think about how their previous fight could have been better. They will learn how to improve for their next battle and will practice those skills over and over again until they become second nature. This will not be the last time you go through something difficult. Hopefully, all of your upcoming seasons of suffering are much less difficult than your previous one. Just in case, make a list of what this battle has taught you, for your future self.

2. Who are you allowing to speak in to your life?

   _____

   _____

   _____

   _____

   _____

   _____

It is nice to have people around you who are compassionate to your suffering, as long as they do not keep you anchored to your past. If you have people in your life who constantly want you to share about your suffering or trauma, you may have to redirect the conversation or spend less time with that person. Some people feed on drama , which may cause them to make you their little pet project. Watch out for these people.

You need constructive, positive people in your life. It is also good to find resources, like books and podcasts that will encourage and build you up.

3. How do you keep your mind in the present moment?

_____

_____

_____

_____

_____

_____

This is a spiritual practice for me. I have to pray every day and ask God to help me find joy in my life without my children. It is a daily struggle. I have seen others dive into work or a project to stay busy enjoying their lives. There are many ways to find joy in your today.

It takes an immense amount of inner strength, time, and may take years to work through your pain and sorrow. Setbacks may occur, but just keep moving forward. Eventually, you will hear yourself laughing again and enjoying your life. You are going to be okay.

Every person working hard to accomplish their goals will experience setbacks. It is natural for old feelings to rise up from time to time, but be sure not to tether your present to your past.

Realize that every worthy goal will offer challenges that must be overcome. When you embark on one of these setbacks, try brainstorming with a friend on how you can find some momentum again. Do something else for a while so you can clear your head. Go on a run, paint a canvas, enjoy a weekend getaway—find something that helps you recharge and refocus.

There are at least a few million books, podcasts, and public speakers out in the world offering advice on how to accomplish your goals. Find a few encouragers, mentors, pastors, or coaches that you like then create a playlist for when you need a mental or spiritual boost. By this time in your suffering journey, you have struggled through and overcome every whisper of negativity that has popped into your head.

You must have a few tricks of your own on how to block out negativity and refocus on what is important. That is what this level is all about. You must find ways to keep yourself focused on the things that matter.

———— •◦• ————

Chapter Eleven

People in Suffering

Watching someone you love
suffer is a very helpless feeling.

–MOM

This chapter is for the people who love and walk with those as they suffer. Let's face it; it's complicated to know how to support or even know what to say to a heartbroken person so here are some suggestions:

The Fixer...

It is better if you do not try to fix the life of a person who is suffering. This is impossible for you, plus it can be an annoyance for the person in suffering. This is a bad habit that many people exhibit. It is an arrogant mindset that comes from a sweet place. Every person on this planet will have a season or two of suffering. It is a process that we have to figure out from the inside out. It is a very personal journey. If you are the type of person who is a fixer, you will be interfering with your friend's healing process.

Giving a hurting friend your attention is the best thing you can give them. Listening allows them the opportunity to process their emotions and feelings. This is very healing. Sitting in silence is also a very loving act. Suffering is a very lonely feeling. Knowing that someone is willing to sit with you is comforting.

Confidentiality...

Never share someone else's private information. Always get your friend's permission if you need to talk to someone about the pain you feel for your friend. It is not unusual to need to talk to someone, but just make sure it's with your friend's permission. It is very important to keep your friend's confidence. Gossiping about your friend's private life can be very detrimental to your friend.

Taking a Break...

Being friends with someone throughout their season of suffering can be challenging. If you need a break, just tell them. Ignoring your hurting friend will only hurt them more. It can take years for your friend or family member to heal from their tragedy or trauma. Take a break; it's allowed! Just tell your friend that you need to recharge a little and you are taking a week's vacation, but you will return in seven days to be all the support they need. You may even try to find someone to fill in for you while you are taking a break.

Just Get Over It...

Be careful to not push someone to be sociable. Sometimes what you think your friend needs is the opposite of what they actually need. It's hard to not push your friend to "get over it," but I assure you that your friend does not want to feel the pain they are feeling. Plus, other people take a lot of energy. Your friend may be using every ounce of their strength to deal with their daily tasks they have to accomplish.

Wise Words...

> If you do not have something nice to say, then do not say anything at all."
>
> –THUMPER'S MOM
> IN THE MOVIE BAMBI

Awkward silence is better than awkward rambling, where confusing words can be taken out of context and you accidentally hurt the person you are trying to help. If the prolonged silence is too uncomfortable for you, pull from your mental hard drive an amusing and interesting story. Everyone enjoys a good story.

Emotional Vomiting...

Try not to dump your problems on a person who is suffering. Find someone else to share with for a while. This is a tricky part of your friendship, because your friend who is suffering still wants to be your friend. It will hurt them to find out you have had struggles that you felt you could not share with them. This requires a balance in letting your friend know that you have some struggles, but you are working on things and everything will be fine. You are keeping your friend in the loop, while not adding on any addition pressure. This is very kind of you. Caring for someone who is suffering is a selfless act.

Physical Contact...

Physical touch is healing. People who are suffering need lots of hugs. I encourage you to be physically nurturing—if it is appropriate, of course. Other ways to show support are cleaning someone's house for them, paying a bill for them, watching their children, doing their laundry, making them a meal, or just sitting and watching a movie with them. The two best sentences to say regularly to someone who is suffering are "What can I do for you?" and "I'm sorry you are hurting."

Prayer...

Remember to pray for your friend often. You can also text them scripture throughout their week. Make them a 4x6 framed bathroom scripture. My bathroom scripture is John 14:27: "Peace I leave with you; my peace I give you. I do not give to you as the world gives. Do not let your hearts be troubled and do not be afraid." I wrote "Enjoy Grace" above it. I read it several times a day when I go to the bathroom.

I have given you several suggestions for how to support your friend or family member in their time of suffering, but never forget to ask, "How can I support you?" Thank you for your selfless act. You will never fully know how kind and necessary it has been.

Internal and External Processors...

People can process grief internally or externally. External processors need to talk things through with someone. Women are commonly external processors. Internal processors do not need or even want to discuss their thoughts, fears, or concerns with anyone. They may throw themselves into their work, spend too

Grieving is a very personal process

much time on a project, or go for a run instead. The grieving process is a very personal one.

How Do You Support an External Processor?

The best way to support an external processor is to listen. An external processor needs someone to listen and lovingly support them in those struggles. Remember the suggestions written above in this chapter—do not try to fix your friend. Listening will do. Occasionally, external processors can become a little obsessive in their need to discuss every thought. This may take more time than you can give.

A support group may be a healthy alternative for your friend. If your friend is not open to a support group, you may have to set some healthy boundaries with them. It is okay to let them know you can only visit during your lunch hour for thirty minutes and after work from 8:30 p.m. until 9 p.m. Sometimes hurting people can be selfish people, so be sure they know how valuable it is to you to be available and how thankful you are to be their support.

I was an external processor throughout our struggle with infertility. I would talk to just about anyone who would listen. I desperately longed for answers, comfort, and reassurance. I learned some very tough lessons about not sharing your personal business with everyone. There were many days when I suffered the consequences of allowing people to speak about my personal life.

One day in particular that comes to mind was when I overheard a coworker complaining about me talking about my miscarriage with one of our clients who had also suffered a miscarriage. My coworker said, "Good grief, is she talking about her miscarriage again?" I was embarrassed and hurt, but eventually learned to process my emotions with only a couple of trusted friends.

How Do You Support an Internal Processor?

Simply being available may not be enough. You may have to be more proactive. Some suggestions for connecting might be to ask if you can join them for a run or help with a project. Your friend may not want to talk about their struggles, but simply making an effort to be around them just in case can mean a great deal.

The occasional text or phone call to see how things are going can be a good show of support for internal processors. Another suggestion is to buy your friend a journal and write, "Always here when you need me" on the front cover page. When in doubt, you can simply ask the internal processor, "How can I be supportive to you during this time?"

On the other hand, there are unhealthy internal processors. These are the people who start showing signs of destructive coping mechanisms. If you suspect that your friend is on a negative path, you must intervene. It is vital for the people closest to this person to stay in communication with one another. All of you will need to discuss a plan in proceeding to get help for your friend if the destructive behavior continues or if any suspicion of suicide arises.

My husband was an internal processor throughout our struggle with infertility. I came to realize he processed his emotions this way after many fights in which I accused him of being emotionless about our situation. In fact, he was hurting just as much as I was, but he threw himself into work and projects to deal with the pain. He got three promotions during this period of his career.

Grieving is such a personal process. There are many ways in which people can grieve. The job of a supporting friend is to simply do that: support them and watch over them. Grieving people can get lost in their pain. Keep an eye on the negative coping mechanisms I discussed previously (e.g., drinking, drugs, negative talk, etc.). And, remember to pray over them often.

Thank you for your willingness to walk with your friend or family member in their time of suffering. We all know this is not an easy task.

———•●•———

Acknowledgements

*T*his is John's (my husband's) story as well. John and I are amazed, thankful, and in total agreement that our marriage survived this journey only by the grace of God. We saw the best and worst in one another during this time. I am so happy we both chose to fight for our marriage. John is my best friend, my faithful warrior, my sexy lover, my traveling companion, and a wonderful blessing to me.

I am immensely grateful for my heavenly Father, who is so very personal to each of us in our suffering. I am thankful we have a God who loves us so dearly. I bask in His grace.

Thank you to all of my family and friends who endured these difficult years with us. Thank you for all of your prayers and your unconditional love.

I would like to give special thanks to my two daring accountability partners. Chasity, you are the truest friend a gal could ever hope for. To my sweet mamasita, thank you for your constant encouragement and courageous truth. I love you both dearly.

———•••———

27698809R00085

Made in the USA
Lexington, KY
02 January 2019